As the Sunflowers Grow.

Stephen Randall

"As the Sunflowers Grow," by Stephen Randall. ISBN 978-1-60264-284-3.

Published 2008 by Virtualbookworm.com Publishing Inc., P.O. Box 9949, College Station, TX 77842, US. ©2008, Stephen Randall. All rights reserved. No part of this publication may be reproduced, stored in a retrieval system, or transmitted in any form or by any means, electronic, mechanical, recording or otherwise, without the prior written permission of Stephen Randall.

Manufactured in the United States of America.

As the Sunflowers Grow.

Sunlight fingers flicker through dawn's awakening curtain,
pours love on our bed of mounting passion alive & thrilling.
As sunflowers grow we lay motionless in a destiny certain,
summer grass sways our bodies soft, delicately touching.

We stare, gaze at floating dandelion seeds in winds away,
two of us free, enriched by the sunrise's hypnotic display.
Our hearts beat fast among golden scenery tasting love,
we admire the cumulus clouds of spiral patterns above.

Together our lives grow stronger, deeper into the year,
green grass bed we now lay upon banishes any fears.
We cultivate our earth; allow seasons to fulfil our wish,
silence breathes into lungs desiring fate to accomplish.

Our sunflower love will grow; reach out to autumn time,
wild seeds we sow on soiled land of passions sublime.
The celestial skies high, colour love's canvas picture,
nature smiles, allows us to fulfil that destiny nurtured.

So near, so far.

Over green hills, mountains sky ceiling high,
love distance miles away, how my soul flies.
You feel so near, close to my troubled heart,
so far away to reach, let our love finally start.

Thoughts, wishes travel roads of sweet dreams,
we meet like two playful actors in a love scene.
The night moon shines, glistens a guiding light,
bright beacons flash, bringing love into sight.

Lonely days pass, fly with gathering speed,
life without you, thorns of a rose that bleeds.
I blow, send gentle kisses to reach your door,
love waves crashing on a beach's pebble shore.

Passion river long twists, turns a tricky passage,
love boat sailing swiftly to your sacred carriage.
I wake, think of you; hope my wishes come true,
my life empty, shallow, how I really need you!

Telephone wire messages flow through my mind,
how I want to hold, caress you, open eyes blind.
Whether near or far, you are always in my heart,
lifting my spirits high, we should never be apart!

Night Serenade.

Twilight falls, wraps its warm evening coat,
enveloping night atmosphere in places remote.
We stroll arm in arm as the sea-shore smiles,
cooling breezes embrace this lovers lane mile.

Lights sparkle, dance on ripple waves moving,
Igniting a star crackle firework orange glowing.
We gaze as the moon guides a passionate way,
soft winds air flow in promenade delight play.

Guitar serenade, music strums love cords strong,
we enjoy, frolic to a festival party all night long.
Time suspended, lost in our own world divine,
love capsules secure, seduced in erotic sublime.

Heart beats jump, dance in long rhythm steps,
gliding feverish bodies to sweet sensuous depths.
Our hands touch, caress as candle lights shimmer,
romance breathes fire ashes reddest hot glimmer.

Eyes stare, eyes glisten moonlight reflection,
lapping up a celebration's compelling devotion.
Desire yearns to play its part in love's charade,
delicate seduction carried by a night serenade.

Love Seasons.

Love flowers blossom, emerge in spring time joy,
entices passion buds to grow among girls and boys.
Sweet petal scents capture, instigate seasonal moves,
fresh lime colour leaves rustle, whisper soft grooves.

Hot summer sun sparkles, shines on naked bodies,
light flicker shadows dancing alive amid green trees.
Two souls float adrift, alone in timeless love serenity,
July's pleasant delightful gift in nature's sanctuary.

September sun lowers in a sky's fading romance,
darkness descends, blights love's final last chance.
Autumn colour display changing to black & white,
love has reached an equinox line burning alight.

Winter icicles lengthen, rain falls deepest snow,
hearts broken in a barren season's loveless show.
Calendar months twist fortunes in aching dismay,
hope rests in the hands of spring's beckoning days!

Voices Echo.

Terracotta floor room memories echo reflective minds,
past remnants time history swirling waves confined.
Old walls wear traces of lives once lived to the full,
smells, odours linger the air in a room's autumn fall.

Doors creak, broken windows sunlight peers through,
wasted years of decorative neglect fade colours blue.
Cold shivers befall the body in tranquil silence,
faint ghost whispers echo a room's empty opulence.

History reminders appear at every corner's turn,
little time capsules portrayed in picture portrait urns.
Cobweb patterns string fill bedrooms a tangled mess,
adding to a home's now long forgotten tired distress.

Tears, laughter rang out loud in party host times,
family, friends alive amid four walls sublime.
Children played up and down spiral wooden stairs,
shouting, smiling in endless days unaware.

Voices echo louder, longer in heartfelt reflections,
memories haunt, linger an old house's dereliction.
Close that door shut, stare misty eyed once more,
past locked away in a mind's treasure box stored.

Let's Swim!

Love finds itself blue ocean water deep,
awakening tired passion fallen fast asleep.
We dive, swim through old rusty wreckage,
answers weary, hidden in coral reef damage.

Come with me! Let's swim among the fishes!
Abandon bad advice; listen to a heart's wishes.
Love ripple waves travel high sea wash tides,
turbulent waters tossing us from side to side.

I watch you slither, slip on a mermaid's suit,
beautiful, elegant vision Mediterranean cute.
You sit on rocks teasing, glisten midday sun,
drawing my senses, play mind games for fun.

Wild horses gallop along excited waves,
liberating us from lost time further astray.
Neptune rises, point's direction way ideas,
we must swim, bathe in blue waters clear.

Aqua lines trace, recognise love emerging,
let's escape misfortune, avoid fate drowning.
Swim into my life! Swim into my open arms!
Let's drift away, believe in destiny's charm!

Winter Rose.

Winter arrives, displays its cold white face,
snow showers darken a sky's vacant space.
Sharp words drop icicle spears in the heart,
winter rose asleep in my love's garden park!

Love stumbles, falls looking for compromise,
January chill freezes the soul sad sorry despise.
The new day sun glistens, reflects love's despair,
willing my red rose to nurture, live without care.

Spring time rose buds alive instigate life,
It thaws sad wintry heart's loveless strife.
Whisper into my ears red vibrant sounds,
speak words vivacious, subtle lines abound.

Hold me in your safe hands of lifelong fears,
banish love streaming pathway's fake tears.
Sweet winter rose shine, become heaven sent,
save a cold heart suffering in lost deliverance!

Human Dysfunction.

Evolution time bomb plays danger game behaviour,
twisted mindsets mistrust thoughts heavily laboured.
Brain cells swirl confused, live a directionless state,
Internet gateway information line decides future fate.

A biological clone resembles mix match of DNA,
science engineers molecules, develops new race.
Black or white skin indicates distinctive birthmark,
we must refrain, ignore medical trials embarked.

Electric wires feed a government lab test leaning,
crazy professors push limits, disregard warnings.
Humans as robots, a reality thrives in quick time,
replacing mankind's century old conditioned lines.

A caveman legacy alive & well in modern ways,
gene generations following blood lines dismay.
To be a black sheep, societies unwanted misfit,
Intellectual hierarchy won't accept the illegitimate.

World of science, modern blessing, dangerous game?
Human biology tampered with test tubes to blame.
Tomorrow's challenges flow like a flooding stream,
breathe dysfunctional notion ending a bad dream!

The River.

Long winding waterway journey travels the land,
crossing green countryside narrow twisty bands.
Snake shaped destination flow tepid and slow,
water reflects, entices sunshine sparkles aglow.

Boats glide; snuggle into a river's gentle ways,
exploring murky water's golden relaxation days.
Sun rays dance glitter patterns summer time fun,
tow path walks enjoyed, restful days high season.

Wildlife lives and breathes an oxygen paradise,
playing, surviving in river ripples soft surprise.
Fish swim; glide among tall green riverside reeds,
ducks camouflaged in canal bank's shadowy trees.

In stillness serene the river explores and delights,
whether early morn dew or starry moonlit nights.
Time passes in slow motion, regresses the soul,
captures life in graceful, meandering water flows.

Father's Tears.

Old man stands alone, eyes full of fate's bitter tears,
tenders his daughter's grave on sanctified land fears.
He sits, kneels before her, face wears pain & sorrow,
mutters silent words, lost hope for life tomorrow.

Mid morning sun beats down, still he stands & stares,
oblivious to the world around him, lives days unaware.
Angels adorn god's monument, protect its chosen one,
soft winds fly a soul to heaven's waiting sacred throne.

Every day and night, whether rain, hail or shine,
father visits his loved one's last resting place shrine.
Silence hangs the air, nature breathes pacified ways,
cold heart holds, seizes a man's meaningless days.

He caresses marble stone, places flowers in deliberation,
forlorn figure, desperate in a morning's faded salvation.
Gentle breezes whisper her name, shiver in shame,
beautiful girl vanquished in reckless behaviour blamed.

Tired & weary eyes, dark shadows late evening display,
sad thoughts collected, kisses her the last time that day.
He leaves, stares at the red sun imploring reasons why?
Head bowed walks disconsolate, waits impatiently to die!

You Make Me Feel!

You make me feel like apple blossom spring,
joy of lambs skipping, birds that playfully sing.
You melt thick ice surrounding a frozen heart,
water long droughts, rescue love swept apart.

When I'm blue, face a thousand wet weekends,
you raise spirits, bring love purple heather sent.
A raging fire burns so incandescent deep inside,
sweeping in hurricanes, there's nowhere to hide.

Time lingers long in your breathtaking presence,
surrounding a heart in aromatic scented essence.
On love lost days, you light a candle flame high,
one smile, eyelash flicker, blue cloudless skies.

You glide towards me, heart skips and hops,
pulse rate record breaking, legs sure to drop.
I'm transfixed, hypnotised by elegance's view,
footsteps gliding gracefully with panache anew.

I feel in perfect harmony, love grows stronger,
hold me! Reassure me! Stay a while longer!
Love connects like bread & wine in life surreal,
fortune colour gold, is how you make me feel!

Concrete Jungle.

Blue clear skyline vanishes in free fall waste,
large concrete blocks built in frenzied haste.
No thought or intelligence to earth's ecology,
man's self destruct mission, destroy geology.

Nothing protected, secure, left naturally alone,
planners instigate demographic pocket zones.
Green fields disappear under material weight,
money driven ambitions, eco-destruction date.

People compacted, sardine space a premium,
attitudes, reasons blinded by profit gain delirium.
Playing fields, football pitches a contractor's greed,
excuses hidden in large corporate money deceit.

Rat race roads filled a million metal machines,
grid lock, anger, going nowhere fast screams.
Layer after layer the concrete jungle spreads,
swallowing lost contours a vast metal bed.

Landscape wears bricks & mortar's darkest cape,
pollution, poison gases prevent human escape.
Blood pen government statistics line future graves,
we require empathy, foresight, a future saved!

Deathly Silence!

The quiet late night hangs a dark chilling silence,
tranquillity surrounds final resting place sufferance.
All around deathly atmosphere eerie and strange,
goose bumps, hair on end, bodies horribly maimed.

Dark shadows walk, furrow among those unaware,
daybreak activity reflects in cat's eyes briefest stares.
Stillness white mist drifts over hills weepy land mass,
occasional moonlight flickers flash signs moving fast.

Deathly silence breathes loneliness fearful night!
Deathly silence lives, instils feelings of fright!

Tense nervous energy drips sweat drops anticipation,
filling air clouds frightened sense of commiseration.
Fear smells blood stains on waiting lined up graves,
false calm after the storm, few young lives ever saved.

Dawn's killing fields hang death on time lest we forget,
aftermath dereliction waves Red Cross flags final regret.
Lost innocent souls flown on white dove wings away,
last walk sunset concludes that sorrowful final day.

Deathly silence breathes loneliness stillest dark night!
Deathly silence remains in fields' fire blaze alight!

Counting the Seconds.

I wait impatiently, count seconds forever slow,
mind runs circles, incandescent red fire glow.
Ever nearer, ever closer to achieving our aim,
longitude, latitude lines a love map arranged.

Fate transported, carried on warm winds fly,
merging love hearts, souls to finally comply.
We live time's mercy, delicate ways lost ship,
minutes of hours join our distant relationship.

Your sunshine illusion greets my waking day,
Instils power, sparkles like a firework display.
We are destined to be freedom birds in flight,
combined together, forever, day and night!

Alive, so alive I search ever deeper inside,
where your smile, elegance lives & resides.
Monday to Sunday, calendar numbers disarray,
I'm counting the seconds till we meet someday.

Walk Away.

Her love's a poison flower bouquet display,
Rose prickle feelings, I just can't walk away.
Time after time I ask the same old questions,
no sure answers satisfy a heart's desperation.

Your surprised voice asks, "why today"?
But I can't live without your special ways.
I miss seeing, talking and being next to you,
one lovely smile turns my grey sky blue!

I live, survive through many silly mistakes,
you make me feel real, alive, hope a vast lake.
Superficial aspects don't interest or please me,
but your sweet nature warms me inside heartily.

I know deep inside I should finally walk away,
leave behind troubles, my constant sad dismay.
It maybe wrong, maybe right, but I do love you,
always have, always will, my love forever true.

Heaven's Smile.

Heaven calls, beckons your broadest smile,
stars glisten, sparkle, welcome you far & wide.
Today's sky shows sadness, moist red eyes,
tomorrow's sun will rise its hill top surprise.

Wings spread, fly a soul to heaven's space,
gliding, carrying this light's eternal grace.
Years so few, years filled with joy and fun,
your spirit fondly touched every setting sun.

Memories linger, remain in the conscience,
kindness, laughter shown with caring patience.
A dream, ambition to succeed, achieve the best,
gentle manners, humour, we were all so blessed.

Red kiss rose sends, flies you far away,
your memory will radiate joy, always stay.
We know somewhere, some bright sunny day,
we will see you smile again, come what may!

Slow Dance.

Rhythm music pulses, jives to night beat time,
guiding, enticing lithe bodies to stretch the line.
Evening romance lingers, captivates sultry air,
drawing seductive glances, passion wind stares.

Slow the music goes, slow movement sequence,
eye to eye grace, ends the evening's deliverance.
Stallion leads his filly to swoop across the floor,
bodies sway, glide as the crowd demands more!

Slow motion mirage colours move left to right,
sequins, pearls sparkle among the strobe lights.
Eyes lock together, dark intense pierces the room,
live statues teasing, alluring, playing their tune.

Like a majestic swan commands still water pond,
dancers liberate, free an audience's unique bond.
Two souls on the floor fill an atmosphere warm,
embracing lovers caress moon light until dawn.

Two step and rumba, glitzy shoes sparkle like fire,
passionate tango swoons, thrills, burns in desire.
The lights softly dim, end pleasure's erotic delight,
silent mannequins leave, drift into the night.

Emotional Waves.

Beauty glides, swoons in emotional waves,
filling my heart soft, sensual lingering days.
Love transported on wash tides slow motion,
red enigmatic smile, demands pure devotion.

A celebration firework sparkling high above,
night Illuminations bright sweetness of love.
Seductive eyes magnetise my sultry senses,
toying with affections, no hidden pretences.

Smooth curves meander, entice male seduction,
rhythmically guide sex's demanding persuasion.
Subtle elegance, grace are dynamic weapons,
large emotional waves sweep over love's season.

An angel face, skin white powder complexion,
empathy radiates charisma in total dedication.
Blanket wave love suffocates suitor's appeals,
wrapped in sea tides washed up deepest thrills.

Soul's Open Window.

Stars shine glitter ball, sparkle the heart,
dejection cuts and scars, tears me apart.
Faith tossed like pebbles along the seashore,
hope vanished in sea mists time ignored.

Spread wings; fly through a soul's window,
breathe, revive a man's love stream slow.
Subtle line symmetry divides love's rules,
marking territory taken forth, actions cruel.

Life's pathway segments of orange pieces,
contentment lost, a feeling nothing pleases.
Come peer at my heart's empty chambers,
window pane reflection, images of danger.

Confused, disorientated, lost in cosmic lines,
clock ticks fast, last chance love cutting fine.
Will you release a heavy burden of shame?
Love patterns complicated, no one to blame!

I light a candle to mark every passing day,
never relinquish hope, you'll blow my way.
As the crow flies, I send a message to you,
step into my soul, believe our love is true.

Vertigo!

Alone I stand to face a steep cliff precipice,
head spins, legs wobble along narrow crevice.
Jekyll & Hyde split personality dually arrived,
fighting one another in past failures contrived.

Spiral twists; loop the loop, I feel dizzy vertigo,
mountain river below awaits body stream flow.
I stare and peer at life's crumbling rocky edge,
fully intent to jump from life's loveless ridge.

Lend me a saving hand, strength of belief,
prevent me ending life, bring lasting relief!
Vertigo rises to the highest mountain peak,
feelings distraught, lacks explanation speak.

Excuses run long like the Mississippi river,
I feel tired and weak, answers undelivered.
I climb higher to reach summit punishment,
head dizzy spins lost pride won't ever relent!

I've lost the will, desire to carry this fight,
cliff edge abyss comes closer within sight.
Life stuck in ruts fearing a mind will let go,
I sink deeper, faster into spinning vertigo!

Café Romantica!

Small Italian café nestles a piazza pavement serene,
aromas wafting the air, young waitress table preens.
Her smile, elegance, gentle movements sweep away,
capture my heart among coffee perfume smells array.

Almond eyes hypnotise amid marble pattern floors,
black & white dress demands attention, mind explores.
You glide everywhere in chess game sequence moves,
delighting customers with beautiful sensual grooves.

Late afternoon sun plays in shadow line guidance,
I sit & dream, enjoy atmospheric life entranced.
I sip a cappuccino watch life pass merrily by,
listen to car horns & laughter as time flies.

Frothy coffee steams beside illumination café parade,
street sings harmony in south Mediterranean display.
Latin lady glides to fill my love cup treacle sensation,
sets a pulse racing with eyelash flickers temptation.

I count pigeons fluttering through the square,
read a newspaper; watch girls with stylish flare.
Time quickly vanishes as I admire you from afar,
heart always yearns for the beautiful café romantica!

Stephen Randall

Clown Man!

Roll up! Roll up! Ladies and gentlemen,
all stand, stare and laugh at this silly man,
he has red faced clothes, wears tearful smile,
happiness is a dream that lives in a place futile.

Fake make-up persona, face masked in sadness,
always searching for affirmation's completeness.
He stands alone a ring of fire, embarrassed times,
relationship history tastes the mouth bitter limes.

Look at him! Laugh at him! What a fool!
Shrivelled figure centre staged, life so cruel.
He notices shaking heads, accusation fingers,
pain failure burns, eats and will forever linger.

I am that clown! Face pale in derisory shame,
I am that clown! Nobody else can I blame.
I will run aground hide my everlasting fears,
I will run aground, drown among my tears!

Among the Rubble.

Night time fears haunt a dark sky ablaze,
piercing sounds scream in a bomb's haze.
Desperate for shelter to escape living hell,
waiting, hoping the noises will be repelled.

Families hold hands for comfort and support,
praying tomorrow ends this needless onslaught.
Aftermath dereliction, smell of devastation bare,
picking up life pieces, feelings of utter despair.

Millions face desolation, future times uncertainty,
all in the blood written name of freedom's liberty.
Long scarred face landscape carries sores deep,
will a new day awaken from a nightmare sleep?

Human intellect vanished in hateful red eyes,
people left hurt, angry a mind's total despise.
Nobody wins in death's needless war abound,
gripped by fright, praying for a saviour found.

Sunlight Smile.

Brightest orange sunrise lifts my fragile soul,
subtle glimpses of sincerity shakes me whole.
If the heart feels blue, frozen in splinter pains,
your smile comforts cold, wet days full of rain.

Touch the heart rainbow colours golden dream,
you save the day, keep our love boat upstream.
Clouds collide when our eyes smile and greet,
bodies shiver; shake delight from head to feet.

Rose scarlet prisms stretch far and wide,
love flies passion seeds floating in the sky.
Your radiant smile invigorates life's decaying hope,
Igniting hot passion sliding on a downhill slope.

Your magnetic smile kisses lips sweet contentment,
allowing sunrays to warm our bodies aching lament.
My life breathes, shines when I see you for a while,
It raises, thrills my heart with your sunlight smile!

A Bright Light!

Throw a dice, lucky number's hidden clue,
back to front apathy strikes home the truth.
I was lost, bewildered, good chances few,
when a light out of darkness in love grew.

You watered, nurtured my desolate flower,
Instigated life, allowed seeds hope of power.
Like the northern star's cosmic force position,
you guided me to a wishing wells' imagination.

In times of disarray, you support my bridge,
strong helping hand along fate's rockiest ridge.
In trouble, despair a light shines from within,
showing me faith, guidance, a belief to win.

Prince of darkness battles good and evil,
fights to decide, realise strength of a devil.
Rain tears fill the heart countless sorrows,
your bright light ensures a better tomorrow!

Soft Whispers.

Daybreak wakens, murmurs a shimmer delight,
hypnotises, encourages passionate fires to ignite.
Sultry lady moves close, eyes demand attention,
breathes subtle whispers, abandons deliberation.

I smell you, feel and taste sugary warm lips,
caressing my body, senses alive hop & flip.
Skin glistens, responds to persuasive ways,
soft words spoken, tantalise, lead me astray.

Sensual kisses jump static line demolition,
fatal moves glide lust sheets natural position.
Water drops drip rhythm sounds to my heart,
Instigating love in gyrating movements start.

Honey! Blow delicate whispers in my ear,
come resurrect, reveal love so crystal clear.
Stay awhile, stay in a love bubble complete,
fill a heart hope, let's drink passion sweet.

Sunlight fingers caress dawn's weary bed,
early morning words dissolve, disappear unsaid.
Come! Come wrap comfort arms relieving pain,
allow soft whispers to dance love's kingdom reign!

Deep inside.

Day and night thoughts submerge quicksand,
recollections lost, so helpless to understand.
Something inside keeps the memory alive,
sad visions of you is a pain that never dies.

Deep inside, burning truths hurt even more,
picture face radiance shines across the floor.
I can't let go! Heart's wrapped in barbed wire,
your smile, grace, arouses my passion desire.

Hot molten love juices flows down a stream,
cups full of hope to drink towards our dream.
I have tried to look away, turn the other cheek,
but I am drawn to your magnetic golden streak.

My heart shivers cold as winter falling snow,
your postures a peacock constantly on show.
It's no use hiding behind lies and pretence,
all I know is inside, no pain is recompense.

Red, Red, Wine!

Dark green bottle sits majestically upon kitchen table,
cherry crimson liquid mixed in variety named labels.
Sunlight catches smooth glass body's perched angle,
red shafts glisten a dust speckle window star spangle.

Relaxation waves of melancholy's consolation glass,
calming sedative to suppress depressed feelings last.
Red wine smiles, comforts a lost soul's devil times,
replacing emptiness, feelings stretch distorted line.

Lights dim as love hands cross an assignation table,
celebration glasses brim full among passion fables.
Candle lit dinners in restaurant night time serenade,
red wine compliant as romance takes centre stage.

Wild corks pop pleasure sounds to a party's loud sins,
behaviour lost in mind game spills latest crazy whims.
Raise a toast, salute health in medicinal prescription,
drink the lords blessed juice, pray for hope salvation!

Faded Time.

Modern world adrift, lost all perspective,
actions spin, collide with no clear directive.
We walk on air, pavements a conveyor belt,
so many things to do, time's ice cream melt.

Sweet lady rushes here, there and everywhere,
multi tasking, juggling errands, going spare!
Days pass like a fast fairground attraction,
commitments pile up, line up in distraction.

How the body and soul needs to get away,
relax, take breath, enjoy those lazy days.
Holidays seem a distant, pleasurable memory,
five minutes alone, read a favourite book's story.

Where has time gone? How do I catch it up?
My clock with no hands, never knows when to stop.
There are no explanations or reason and rhyme,
I live from day to day in confused faded time!

Love whispers.

Hush! Hush! Sweet girl, look all around,
voices talk whispers touching the ground.
Trees rustle leaves in excited bold moves,
earth movement sends love in spiral truths.
Is it your love whispers?

Moonlight shadow, moonlight casts a gaze,
your words swirl, twist like a giant maze!
I walk confused, disorientation takes hold,
trying to gather senses lost, disillusion bold.

Open ears to acclaim, desire subtle virtues,
listening to every noise, face a static statue.
Wind hopes carried on passion required,
breezing into my life, wrapped in desire.
Is it your love whispers?

Compass point north, south, east and west,
drawn to your magnetism, a man possessed.
I search high and low through driving snow,
wishing for a light shining love hearts aglow.

Skin Deep.

There's no disguise, pain cuts deep inside,
surface senses sliced, with nowhere to hide.
Sad rejection digs, burrows holes bone deep,
scars refuse to heal, eyes awake never asleep.

Faith fades a final flickering candle light,
last chance hope hidden in the darkest night.
Knock loud on heaven's door to enter passion,
release frustration, allow our romance fruition.

Skin deep accusations litter love's dire street,
lost, bewildered in wet wandering disbeliefs.
Turn your back; bury me in a loveless grave,
please accept explanations, past times forgave.

Life balances on the longest, thinnest tight rope,
spiralling in confusion, leads to uncertain hope.
Whatever you say, my heart continuously seeps,
but the pain is always more than just skin deep!

Celebration Temptation.

It's party time, ignore moral consequences!
Live life to the full, lose controlling mind senses.
Adolescent behaviour, attitudes mirror despise,
glasses full, no holds barred, no compromise.

Youth society attitudes spiral, disregard blame,
debonair ladies cloned into masculine shame.
Intelligent people reckless, seemingly unaware,
street shouting, swearing, abusive without care.

A waste, sacrifice of healthy intelligent minds,
Friday, Saturday round robin public house times.
Have we become aliens among a civilised race?
Girls, boys sick on pavements, gutter bed place.

21st century party game, drink/drug cocktail,
displays immaturity, bang a coffin's final nail.
Temptation, friends insist you follow the rules,
hospital outcome, your turn among the fools!

Dignity stripped, a police cell for your bed,
concussed, delirious, totally lost your head.
What financial health cost in money terms?
Life tossed in the air, the soul slowly burns.

Climate Woes!

Historical data lists, records show warning signs,
earth under attack, reckless actions of mankind.
A planet's rapid face change in ecological ways,
Ice melts, droughts & monsoons reveal dismay.

Are humans the red devil in god's creation?
Pollution, destruction and culpable rich nations.
Water levels rise, landscape slowly disappears,
we need political honesty, solutions vividly clear.

Scientists study reams of information collated,
giving conflictive reasons to earth's time dated.
Machinery, smoke cloud emissions gone astray,
Indicates insane use in a planet's golden days!

Seasons have altered geographic isobar positions,
winter warmer, summer hotter, a false condition.
Today's woes need a new train of meteor thought,
will the past rescue the future's timeless fraught?

Industrial revolution's see-saw manufacture time,
provided work, wealth along demographic lines.
Are theories hocus-pocus, a misinterpreted game?
Will the outcome be natural or man's great shame?

Stephen Randall

Vanished into Thin Air.

My house lives, breathes, but is empty,
inner walls require your serene empathy.
Lightning fast you abandoned love's home,
tearful desolation leaves me feeling alone.

Where are you? Why did you go?
Disappeared quickly like melting snow.
My mind turns cartwheels round & round,
cries for help, fists thumping the ground.

Days bright and sunny cloud skies dark,
sun hides away, ignores dawn's happy larks.
Words of advice, false hope lives dismay,
I don't hear or listen, intelligence disobeys.

I hunted, searched, left no stone unturned,
hands sore, bloody in constant painful burns.
Vanished into thin air, no sign or clue remains,
tears flow a river, drowning my heart in pain.

Where have the sacred birds of justice flown?
Blood wire guilt, anger, words speak in moans.
Fly back to me! Taste forgiveness, however grave,
I will pray to the heavens, hope our love is saved.

New horizons?

Winds of change whistle wildly in my mind,
follows a guiding light where fortune shines.
An open blue crystal sky with visions pristine,
alters spectrum colours in hallucination dreams.

Sparkling horizon reflects your sunny smile,
lighting all it touches in sunbeams for miles.
Why are you so distant, further out of reach?
Like a survivor washed up on a lonely beach.

To run and hide, deny bright visionary future,
meet harsh challenges, colour this blank picture.
Our planets of love require symmetrical lines,
why are thoughts, actions, curiously maligned?

Distant sun glows on a face in sparkling rays,
light blinding dizziness, clouding the new day.
Night time stars glitter, dazzle true fascination,
easing feelings of continuous consternation.

Life's many challenges appear like hot springs,
Inducing sounds, noises of church bells rings.
Look ahead; try to meet your fate head on,
fresh day brings the chance of a new horizon!

Other Side.

What dark grave secrets could be true?
Life after death, a reincarnation new!
Theories appear staking wildest claims,
logical answers mysteriously unexplained.

Mortal coil questions, who? What are we?
Peer into our ancestors' distant family trees.
A blind search to reveal a million lost years,
hope there is a next life, disregard any fears.

What's on the other side, paradise or hell?
Revelations a holy grail confused deep well.
Forlorn desire to greet loved ones again,
share tears, laughter and make amends.

White shadow ghost hangs over a grave,
cold wind chill walks on someone to save.
Time zone lapsed world forever unknown,
ancient earth full of broken skull and bones.

No time for regression, look into a deep past,
the here and now is what we must make last!
Other side comes to us all, one final black day,
maybe it's better, dark secrets remain that way!

Dot to Dot Pattern.

White sheet paper, blank empty lines,
love pathway a Morse code secret design.
Romance stringed out in black dots deranged,
picture hidden, disguised in invisible ink strange.

Join up the pattern, realign where love failed,
colour a relationship forever lost and dispelled.
Life's template changes with constant confusion,
mysterious lay lines criss-cross in bad disillusion.

Come stop this gyrating world we have created!
Puzzle pieces tossed in the air simply repeated.
Follow your heart, release apprehension you bare,
A to Z map becomes clear, contour segments aware.

Dot to dot seems to be our lives permanent state,
reflection, hindsight reminders of love desperate.
Take time to examine, join dot patterns completion,
allow love to unite through our time's lost transition!

Rain Tears.

Cold winter shiver drops awash my face,
touching white skin pale lines fateful trace.
Tear rain spots fall, fly the wind's disarray,
dissolves understanding leads the heart astray.

River water travels, passes through lost minds,
hoping for a saviour hand to rescue love blind.
Pain, hurt fills the soul tough challenging ways,
absolution, redemption vanished in distant days.

Rain salt tears taste the mouth full of surprise,
your perfume handkerchief wipes my wet eyes.
Dry land relief wind you bring, offer in haste,
salvation gift presented, rectify timeless waste.

Desert oasis lady forgive mistakes however grave,
my inner yearning & desire deserves to be saved.
Tears no longer well, fall down my saddened face,
your love and kindness shines in eternal grace!

Jekyll and Hyde.

I am right you know, always have been!
Ideas better than yours, top of the scene.
You think you're great, an impressive man,
convictions deluded, actions without plans.

Listen to me, open eyes; I'm top of the tree,
first past the post, a winner, can't you see?
You're a dreamer, self-righteous to a fault,
reckless decisions, force of a thunder bolt.

I made judgements in faith, total honesty,
If I don't get a knighthood, it'll be a travesty!
You're a liar, cheat, disgrace to one and all,
only you can't see, notice the biggest fool.

Look I've explained, shouted until I was ill,
I don't accept criticism, never have, never will.
That's typical, characteristic, you arrogant man,
listen to opinions, advice, try to understand

Well its goodbye, farewell, I've done my best,
my legacy assured, history will decide the rest!
Yes, it is farewell, better late than never,
Jekyll & Hyde persona, weak as a feather!

Who are we?

Centuries old theories swirl in mystery time,
past mislaid in mystification relics divine.
Ancient tabloids reveal stories of our forebears,
large depth of knowledge in periodical despair.

To trace, research our disjointed family trees,
searching to solve biological secrecy disease.
Constant regression, obsession to find legacies,
will it satisfy, gratify a mind's speedy curiosity?

Today bears no resemblance, enlightens the past,
have we progressed, learned our lessons at last?
Civilisation speed travels at technological pace,
engineering feats of yesteryear, a fading grace.

We must thank the pioneer's foresight beliefs,
their intelligence outweighs impoverished disbelief.
How far can we go into undiscovered conventions?
Will future achievements surpass historic inventions?

Tomorrow's child in revolution inspired confidence,
carries hopes and dreams to make a difference.
History repeating itself is a message we must learn,
kindness, warmth, put war in a past that won't return.

Midnight Walk.

I toss, turn; anxiety causes deprivation sleep,
worries compound the mind, seriously deep.
I make a coffee, turn on the television,
It's no good; I'm full of guilty derision.

I leave the house, set off for a long walk,
streets dark, midnight silence I eerily stalk.
I pace up and down, thinking of a way out,
cold night air shivers, there's nobody about.

Answers run away like a scared urban fox,
running to safety, an alleyway corner box.
I count steps, trace cracks in the pavement,
still no solutions allow me time to repent.

A lonely walk with no obvious master plan,
full moon shadow steps, nobody understands.
I stroll, hunt around a 24 hour shopping store,
wasting time, searching answers unexplored.

I return home no nearer finding the truth,
early hours still quiet, dark a silent mouth.
A midnight walk hasn't helped find answers,
daybreak will soon arrive, I feel no better!

New Dawning.

Green fresh morn resplendent in first light,
awakens wide eyed, leaving behind twilight.
Early dew glistens, sparkles gem diamonds,
wetting nature's thirst drops of Lilly ponds.

Sun begins its daily venture in beckoning sky,
opening earth's curtain to daybreak's noisy cry.
The grass shimmers, announces its welcome,
rhythm dancing in morning time kingdom.

Orange colour canvas in sleepy eyes perceive,
tantalise, excite love heart's sentimental sleeve.
The soul sighs, greets its new day's best friend,
warmth, gentle feelings wish for time suspend.

White mists dissolve in glorious, enchanting days,
Invigorating senses in aromatic blossom displays.
Breathe, taste and smell life's pleasure unique,
Instigating lively passion on earth's time antique.

Dawn chorus singing birds line a hedges seat,
free morning musical festival is nature's treat.
Red, yellow colour rainbow displays adorn,
such beauty witnessed on a summer's morn!

I will be there!

When the dawn sunrise starts a new day,
brings life to earth's constant dismay,
I will be there!
When the sky weeps tears of sadness,
wraps my heart in painful loneliness,
will you be there?

In times of joy, happiness and fun,
flower colour display in god's kingdom,
I will be there!
When I need love, hope and security,
hands to hold me, save me in infinity,
will you be there?

In this world so full of hate and despise,
no common sense or will of compromise,
I will be there!
Whether spring, summer, autumn or winter,
hot sun, cold frost of icy water splinters,
will you be there?

When I'm old, weak I will be there!
If I need your love will you be there?

High wire love.

Balancing high, dangling free in love's sky,
mindful decisions shake, disturb and go awry.
Reasons freeze, sneeze in cold fearful realisation,
actions live a fragile wire frayed in complication.

Thoughts spin, swirl like an uncontrollable kite,
twisting difficulties black & white, day & night.
A barefoot dash through emotional hot coals,
dance on fire, so many stories remain untold.

Passion, desire drives wild ideas and notions,
frivolous senses paralysed in reckless devotion.
Auburn, blonde and black hair it's all the same,
I'm like a child in denial, refuse justifiable blame.

High wire love I live, breathe will surely destroy,
self-righteous feelings tumble in deceptive ploys.
I plunge in deep ravines, canyons of guilty despair,
selfish love, affections collide high mountain stairs!

Shiny Metal Toy.

Colour treasure beacon shines on a drive,
gleaming metal box, a honeycomb bee-hive.
Pride and joy, essential member of the family,
wild vibrant colours adorned, admired endlessly.

You treat it with care, diligence and kindness,
clean, polish every inch, leisure time weakness.
Important to lazy days, a spare pair of limbs,
sociable times, friends ride on childish whims.

You furnish, decorate interior designs flair,
furry dice, strange animals stuck everywhere.
Wheel spins, smoke curtain on devil's ride,
racing next model, engine power race slide.

Drive narrow country lanes, hair flow eyes,
dust, noise, scaring older drivers to despise.
A mean machine partner to enjoy to the end,
speeding around corners, tight scary hairpins.

Turn the key, slip on a cd, listen to loud music,
leave behind life stresses, a real electric tonic.
Freedom veins flow, chariot drive everywhere,
fast car taking you on wheels to heaven's chair.

Ladies Handbag.

Feminine mystery encapsulates confined space,
unique object to clutter a woman's refined place.
A strange, secret world inside, witnessed alone,
contents guarded fiercely like a dog with a bone.

Tardis space interiors, everything has its place,
make up, mirrors and personal cosmetic grace.
Labyrinth cave of ladies dark unknown secrets,
world far too complicated for any man to upset.

An essential life support, accessory, third hand,
what pleasures lay inside we'll never understand.
Lady powders her nose, mirror checks pencil liner,
bag refined, resplendent in flash leather designer.

Where would they be? How could they live without?
Magic box of tricks, men want to scream & shout.
Beware! Never pry or ask for a sensible reason,
ladies handbag complicated as the four seasons!

Springtime.

Early morn dew drops sparkle in first light sun,
opening the new day in April's delightful season.
Nature buds awaken, rise from winter's long sleep,
smiling, uplifting our hearts long awaited treat.

Colour scale shades wrap, cover rolling landscapes,
fresh apple, cherry perfume pictures that decorate.
Trees wave their branch arms in ceremonial cheer,
Inviting us to step into spring's joyful delicate air.

Free time strolls in country lanes golden trails,
breathe fragrances invigorating a soul compelled.
Bird song fills the atmosphere cacophony sounds,
orchestral vibrations in musical notes dumbfound.

May's light green shade captures spring's essence,
slowly ventures forth into summer's waiting presence.
An annual festival arrives with invariable surprise,
once tasted never forgotten from sunset to sunrise.

Telepathic Sensuality!

Distant communication line strings far and wide,
electric shocks jump in telepathy wires disguised.
I close my dreamy eyes, think of you here with me,
thoughts falling, floating from love's autumn tree.

Senses alive, breathing passion to come into view,
how I want to feel, touch, taste your sensuality true.
Heart beats faster, faster in lust tracks destination,
body yearns, desires our blessed union to fruition.

I lay my weary, sleepy head, bed empty and cold,
dreams float, spiral sky high in stories unresolved.
So alone, alone and tired of destiny's tight grip,
soul drifts abandoned like a storm wrecked ship.

Signals I transmit relay to my love on distant shores,
If she could hear, read them, how the mind implores.
Forlorn longing seizes every commonsense eventuality,
my head lost in mind pulses of telepathic sensuality!

Pretty as a Picture.

You're so beautiful, articulate and pretty,
lighting up darkness, making hope a reality.
Strong presence, aura, sowing wild seeds,
confuse sensibilities, impossible to read.

Apple tree orchard bears fruits of your name,
soaking up sunshine, summer's radiant game.
You walk on water, part love's raging seas,
bring serenity, joy swimming among disbelief.

Pretty as a picture, fragile, delicately serene,
powerful magic spell cast over my day-dreams.
You breathe love, sweetness, when I'm down,
comfort me; restore faith to an ageing clown.

Portrait gallery, eyes full of staring people,
high on a pedestal, taller than a church steeple.
Everybody stands hypnotised by subtle grace,
one in a million looks, picture perfect face.

If only I could steal, capture a vacant heart,
banish solitude, longing, let romance start.
Your beauty glides in view of wishful dreams,
swan grace elegance crossing a tearful stream.

Life's Jigsaw.

Mixed up pieces live on a distorted line,
life's complications form shapeless time.
Square pegs in round holes rule the day,
right place, wrong time, constant dismay.

Lack of symmetrical lines jagged and tall,
our ideas disjointed, life a confusing stall.
Sharp edges cut deep, blocking future way,
relationships falter, divorce ending dismay.

Reproduction pressure, continue family tree,
financial disarray, youthful sterility fading plea.
Age concerns restrict human biology timetables,
turning back the clock, retrieve test tube labels.

Life's gamble, the right slot, wrong money,
one arm bandits' lucky chance, never funny.
Our strange jigsaw life unshaped & unclear,
to rearrange in serenity so incredibly rare!

On Reflection.

Time moves on never stopping for breath,
attitudes considered right, face certain death.
To regress, reflect back on past selfish ways,
climb ivy walls; deny the hurt of past days.

Delve into hindsight try alter mistakes broken,
rectify problems, alter callous words spoken.
Love walls close in ever higher, ever faster,
suffocating hope, like an unavoidable disaster.

Echo chambers barren, cold scare of inner soul,
reverberates sounds that haunt, bad times untold.
Cracked mirror reflection a shadow out of shape,
disguised, hidden in love's black heavy cape.

Two hearts in collision, meet on a star bright,
dancing, darting in a moon dust speckled light.
On reflection, we should have changed our ways,
the future is a reminder of past immature days.

Chain Linked.

365 days of ecological cycle dose unknown,
problems, challenges arise the weight of stone.
Life's plastic expense driven materialistic ways,
hands chained together, slave souls led astray.

Line after line we follow government red tape,
desperate to relinquish a stranglehold's escape.
Bad luck, misfortune, eyes caught closed unaware,
hole gets deeper, solutions surrounded by despair.

Fooled, tricked, crooked smile so hard to believe,
sign here, there's no fear, one & one makes three.
Financial burden linked, chain weight heavy tons,
you want more, need more, borrow money for fun.

What status are you? Where do you come from?
Silver spoon, old school tie brigade conundrum.
Working class man tied to the chain gang's walk,
gazing blindly into the distant sun, unable to talk.

Farmhouse water wheel turns constant circles,
cold water runs over hot chains, frozen icicles.
Life is what you make it, flip a coin, wait and see,
day after day breathe stale air, same old company.

Comfortable.

Feelings, reasons arrive like wispy clouds high,
emotions carried along on soft winds long sigh.
Explanations lose voice in storm force gales,
I'm comfortable with you, my heart set sails.

Words tumble, mumble trip over the tongue,
lost for inner breath like a love tune unsung.
I sit; stare at your radiant glowing facade,
dreaming of a life devoid of love's charade.

Reflections circle the mind in answers true,
my soul feels at ease, a song bird that flew.
Let sacrifices be worth their weight in gold,
our love story is waiting eagerly to be told.

Safe & sound, wrapped in protective fabric,
bond between us, a live-wire electric static.
I promise devotion, bring passion to the table,
allow my open heart to make love comfortable.

Flower Joy.

Bright and vibrant, nature's eyes wide open,
sparkle spectrum display as a new day begins.
Aromatic air seduction, bubbles float to tease,
pollen smells drift on imagination's love trees.

To lovers, friends, flowers portray love & peace,
sweet joyful symphony on a magic golden fleece.
Flowers revel in summer's colourful manifestation,
bringing inner warmth, joy in perfume sensations.

A gift of appreciation to a lover's last appeal,
signature tune plays sweet on voices revealed.
Window ledge flaunts its bouquet rainbow show,
carnations, roses, wide smiles on faces aglow.

In times of war they show respect & grace,
beautiful, illuminating light in a barren place.
Flower's faith healing qualities shine so bright,
soothes aching hearts, every day and night.

Fire and Water.

Fire blazes, raging fire burns and spits inside,
Instant relief desired, required, long on the rise.
Burning fierce, it burns me up into hot ashes,
spiral smoulders hang the sky in storm flashes.

Body heat explosive glows bright red hot,
come bring a love water relief, never stop!
My soul a beach, wide open to the elements,
send empathy on wings, let my heart lament.

Life continues among fire question hypocrisy,
leaves me incomplete, washed up in mediocrity.
Heat, white searing heat scorching to the touch,
your love needs to ride waves desired so much.

As the smoke drifts clouds away distant hope,
my heart on wheels sprints a downhill slope.
Fire and water, romances mixed up mystery,
collides, combines, lives through our history.

Dark Demons.

Painful anguish sways tall columns high,
feelings manifest as hurt lines swirl inside.
Day after day we battle red demon sores,
fight woeful sorrow, behind closed doors.

A brave exterior hides hurting truth within,
Inferiority complex rises, breaks thin skin.
Hopes drown in river stream currents fast,
I'm underwater, submerged in regret's past.

Nobody knows what saddens a weak heart,
failing people kind, tearing the soul apart.
Future happiness is to break a vicious seal,
light glowing saviour, love of someone real.

Dry sand desert longs for a rain cloud sky,
release drought parched land with floods cry.
Heart frozen, time unforgiving in its icy lament,
escape, evade decisions in wasted years spent.

Depression hangs like a damp thick sea mist,
suffocating, repressive, confiscates a pessimist.
To battle demons, find the real person lost inside,
turn back the clock, change misdemeanour times.

Love on fire.

Snow filled skies hide destiny's sun,
searching for love, heart come undone.
A glimmer, slither of hope shines bright,
love fires burn an orange radiance night.

Sweet brief moments, eyes speak harmony,
trace line movements glide perfect symphony.
Eyelash flicker ignites passion's teaming rain,
two hearts on fire, warming cold heart's pain.

Questions unanswered, refuse the obvious,
together we can ride storms heavily curious.
Floor covered with carbon ash love remains,
read letters sprawled, spells out our names.

Seductive chemistry between us will never die,
we accept reality with our soul's flying high.
Cupid arrows' final message to aching hearts,
let's reincarnate hot ashes, wheels of love start.

Sun blessed.

Bright yellow ball sky high, king of planets,
galaxy controller of earth's moving orbits.
Hot universal life cycle, burning eternally,
dictating the weather, climates universally.

Earth's father eye guides are daily fiction hold,
hot and cold patterns conspire, become untold.
A god worshipped or despised in various climes,
drying the land, welcome relief in monsoon times.

The sun's hypnotising power to the human race,
sun tan lover's, skin bronzing, old wrinkled face.
A blinding ball of fire, commands an obedient sky,
religious symbol to ancient races, master on high.

Sunrise excites, warms the heart constant smiles,
electric surge vitamin D, long shadows on sundial.
Whether adored, deplored, our sun remains king,
orchestrating our lives, decides the future it brings.

Hurting heart.

Ship wreckage floats a sea's fierce night storm,
I am tossed aside, rag doll treatment the norm.
My feelings are deep, painful don't you know?
Wild accusations, lies feel cold as driven snow.

Scratch below thin surface to reveal true hurt,
broken toy you're bored with, buried in the dirt.
You judge a book by its cover, ignore contents alive,
flick through old dusty pages, see sentences thrive.

Wipe away salt tears; reveal a man's disguise,
crying out, reaching for kindness lost paradise.
Long journeys to a cold heart have no ending,
believe in time, I can heal your inner hurting.

One day you may have to reappraise actions,
my flesh & bone stripped, no true satisfaction.
Release pent up emotions, bursting to be free,
let love's restriction, suffocation finally breathe.

Fast Rat Race.

I stand and stare in reams of constant disbelief,
people cloud hopping, too busy for timely relief.
Head down, full steam ahead, their on a mission,
must meet deadlines; avoid boss's eye suspicion.

First past the post, large bonus cheque in view,
don't stop me! I must tow the company line true.
Flash suit, smart dress, must catch the MD's eye,
suck up, lick shoes to climb corporate ladder high.

Twenty hour days, no breaks ease a treadmill,
no time for family or friends cash a drug thrill.
Designs on retiring early, blind a junior's ideals,
too much work, no play to enjoy all the spills.

A BMW, Mercedes Benz, I'm worth money!
Who cares if hands are full of sticky honey?
Chase the rainbow, find a pot of fortune gold,
risking health in black economy plots untold.

The rat race gets faster day by challenging day,
working man deceived by director's fat cat ways!
When the wheels finally come to a juddering halt,
who will take the blame, admit it was their fault?

Hanging by a Thread.

Love bewilderment dismissive, so submissive,
vortex spiral emptiness disfiguring lost minds,
twists and turns burn, strangle all our positives,
hanging by a thread, desperate thoughts unkind.

Walk the plank, duck pond dip water strife,
answers swallowed in reeds tangled design,
no clues, ideas can escape this devil's knife!
Left out to dry, forgotten sad lonely valentine.

Walk hollow eyes searches pavement cracks,
voices proclaim, denounce outcomes deranged,
our lives transpire, an off-line runaway track,
A to Z Street map vanished in fate lines changed.

Time lingers, hangs on love's frayed despair,
forgiveness reluctant to unify a dream's desire,
we persist in vain, ideas forever live unaware,
passion denied in disorderly threads conspired.

Out of Reach.

My life a moving pavement of escalator steps,
up and down conveyor, decisions totally inept.
I run before walking, speak with a false tongue,
risking bad consequences, waiting to be hung.

Fulfilment, happiness seems far out of reach,
like a stowaway stranded on a deserted beach.
Time is cruel, reckless in anti-clockwise motion,
trips up plans, demolishes good idea notions.

A lost soul gazing into love's darkest ravine,
trying to reclaim enthusiasm's fallen dream.
Fortune cogs stuck in square wheel fashion,
colours black & white, head craves passion.

Your safety, rescue fades far in the distance,
hiding, unwilling for love to seize a final chance.
Upside down, right to left, there's no direction,
can our lives ever obtain a solid connection?

It's the Walk.

Lady eroticism entices male predilection,
feline sexy steps glide elegant distraction.
Legs shimmer; shake teasing stylish flare,
grabs the attention, wide eyed gasp stares.

Catwalk parade, fashion colour delights,
It's the walk of sultry male induced strife.
Flick of hair, feet glide to silent dance,
walk of love, eyes of a heart in a trance.

It's the way you move, poetry in motion,
hypnotised pendulum swing sheer devotion.
Lady divine, angel delicate wings bright,
beauty displayed in peacock feather delight.

Silk dress design lines implode the mind,
clinging to body shape, open eyes blind.
Tall, slender temptress steals the heart,
paradise steps tear an aching soul apart.

Summer day's provocative colour show,
every man drawn, transfixed, faces aglow.
Hips move rhythm heart beat on overdrive,
traps masculine senses in a honey bee hive.

Unashamed.

Take my hand, come closer, don't be shy,
I live, breathe, sleep under the same sky.
Emotions, sentiments face gun barrier walls,
eyes speak pacifist, voice in desolation calls.

Don't be ashamed, afraid of sore appearances,
my heart beat senses life's helpless resistance.
Dry shelter, warm bed, western comfort's norm,
let compassion rise, rescue a soul's thunderstorm.

A people's disease afflicts, scares naïve minds,
understand, realise what's under a surface blind.
Somebody help, alleviate needless suffering!
wipe tear stains, erase a nations' capitulation.

Reluctance, hesitating for a better tomorrow,
dignity lost, pride swallowed in selfish sorrow.
Birds circle blood red skies over burial fields,
stripping remains of death's dirty soil yields.

Dusty road covers tracks to hells' waste ground,
dry and barren earth, water nowhere to be found.
God's forgotten brothers, sisters pleading hands,
cruel civilisation reality, people don't understand.

Release me!

Awash with decisions, pressing ideas,
guide me, show me how I overcome fear.
I struggle with withering, wilted inner belief,
help me colour this picture, provide relief.

A weight of guilt only you can relinquish,
lift my soul, take my hand, never vanquish.
Life littered with scattered broken wishes,
come swim with me among the shoal of fishes!

Drifting, meandering along a flowing stream,
touch my heart, soothe the pain in lost dreams.
A spark that lies between us so strong & pure,
soft fated winds lifting, demanding to explore.

My persecuted soul will forever ache & shiver,
take the reins of chance for passion to deliver.
As time passes shadows lengthen and darken,
take my heart and mind let our senses sharpen.

Release me from heavy chains movement restricts,
breathe fresh life into passion times that contradict.
Alone we can travel, navigate dark mysterious seas,
old gypsy travellers on long roads roaming free!

Stephen Randall

Look the other way!

Please don't hide, look away from me!
I'm the same flesh & bones underneath.
Skin colour shade in variations unique,
touch me, feel me, hear me breathe.

Don't be scared, frightened of my colour,
I desire, believe in life's unified honour!
Take a knife, cut deep into fleshy skin,
I do bleed red blood, banish racist sins.

Mother tongue diverse, country lives fear,
recognise, accept these words honest tears.
We breathe and walk in perilous street times,
faces stark, witness discrimination party lines.

Perceive, open blind acceptance, I'm no stranger,
I need a future, home in a land free from danger.
Pleas you've heard before knock at border doors,
sanctuary, hope for a better life, walk golden floors.

Sorry eyes tell a story, reveal inner soul torture,
journey over land and sea, reach a safer future.
Look at me! I am human, don't you want to see?
I suffer this painful, dreadful life because I believe!

Airport Madness.

It's holiday nightmare time, endless delays,
hot-head frustration building, faces of dismay.
I stare constantly at the flight board static,
my eyes popping, figures smaller automatic.

An impatient wait for news, time clock ticking,
every year same situation, tiring and infuriating.
I look at my watch, time forever stands still,
go for a cup of coffee, moan aghast at the bill.

Endless security measures posted everywhere,
Strip bone naked, empty pockets, going spare.
Passengers roaming, circling anxiously around,
long faces of red thunder, head scratching frowns.

Next year I will change my travel destination,
I'm fed up glued to this seat, a no-win situation.
At last a voice calls us to gate 113 so far away,
I try to move, legs go numb, what a lousy day!

Are You Listening?

Voices shout louder, longer, never stop,
running circle pains, head spins and throbs.
Is there anyone out there who really cares?
Words lose breath, meaning, stripped bare.

I'm falling, tumbling in vacuum suction hell,
love's candle flame flickers its final farewell.
Fresh face angel, come save my desolation,
lift a broken soul, show me complete devotion.

Tap drips faster, louder in nightmare dreams,
I wake in cold sweat, scared of loud screams.
A long flowing satin dress crosses lines plain,
leaving an impression, love hopes lost in vain.

Pin drop shatters night silence in shady love,
realisation it's hopeless, we need faith above.
Maybe its right, maybe its wrong, who knows?
I just want you to listen, let love swim and flow.

Reading the Signs.

Love walks blind, ignores danger calls,
forever dazed, mystifyingly enthralled.
My aching head spins lost in dark clouds,
high voices shout advice clear and loud.

Blinkered, I run towards a thick sea mist,
forgetting all reasons, never top of my list.
Indications, revelations, I turn a blind eye,
has your love signals been pie in the sky?

My stamina weakens, saps withering energy,
rash actions treated like a burning sad effigy.
Send me, lend me, show love flashing bright,
I read your mind, hope to get the green light.

Flash bulb hill beacon calls my aching heart,
love signals telling us we will never be apart.
Reading right signs a complicated expedition,
let's seize the moment, bring love to fruition!

Death's Eye.

Mortal coil time knocks on destiny's door,
fate concealed dates, circumstances ignored.
White gown vision beckons you into next life,
bright lights drawing senses, relieving strife.

A backbone shiver, death's eye comes in view,
black shadow silhouette, apparition smoke blue.
The next life's mysterious Holy Grail paradise,
non-believers scornful, reject theories deride.

Fables, yarns of yesterday's wisest prophets,
leave clues, insights to today's beliefs derelict.
Coded scriptures, symbols depict ancient tales,
Indicating intelligence, ancestor's magic spells.

Ruby eyes shine; capture the mind's attention,
staring at death's premature, grave acceptation.
Mind plays tricks in sub-conscious dream sleep,
death's eye watching us, too afraid to weep!

Disillusionment!

Tease looks entice a soul open and bare,
powerless to oppose, held forever in despair.
My face a newspaper headline shouting loud,
heart disappointed, lost in a madding crowd.

Avert love gazes if you choose, I feel no ill,
flick blue eye shadow lids, love's bitter pill.
Shiver me; leave a taste honey bee sweet,
drift, float into a mind, make life complete.

Puzzle pieces trail in lines derelict despair,
danger in perilous beauty, actions unaware.
A moon dust mist, magic sprinkle of love,
fly into my life, elegant white feather dove.

Don't go, relinquish heaven time on earth,
stay a while; let's ride tidal waves of truth.
Revisit hope sinking titanic speed disaster,
let me be a servant to your slavish master.

Relationship threads frayed, torn to shreds,
no point in fighting, accept what lies ahead.
Mars meets Venus, Roman gods' lost dream,
unified in commitment, subtle times serene!

Do I belong?

Something weird, strange bothers me,
events surrounding, multiply by three.
I look at today's youth, fashion thrills,
nothing seems right, fits my mind's ideals.

Time flashes by, races at lightning speed,
maybe I have turned into a man of tweed?
Modern clothes, haircuts and wild behaviour,
appear at odds with my sensible demeanour.

I sound like my father, moaning and groaning,
man made eternal pessimist, without warning.
I hate to see streets filthy, smelling of decay,
bad language, ignorance constantly displayed.

I feel stuck in the middle, an alien in a crowd,
speechless, bewildered, sights crazy and loud.
Respect, manners are what I need to appease,
humanity and kindness are reluctantly seen.

A solution, resolution to clean bad smog air,
why do so few stand up, say they do care?
Maturity brings sarcasm gathering at pace,
I feel like a stranger with a tired old face.

Friction Addiction.

Compulsive actions thrive, ride an addiction,
anger flies in the face of relationship friction.
Apathy's tired years, comfy slipper syndrome,
taking each other for granted, unstable home.

We argue and fight, resolutions last miracle,
splinters dig deep in life's tired vicious circle.
Blame culture rises high, touches tearful skies,
feelings shallow, unforgiving, nothing is right.

You don't want to leave, don't want to stay,
life a tragedy scene in a Shakespeare play.
Family guilt trip, knowing right from wrong,
you can't leave, sense of duty pulls strong.

Why do we hurt the people we love most?
Sacrifice good for bad, disregard the cost.
Friction between us grows deeper every day,
hateful accusations cause permanent disarray.

You can't live with, can't live without,
differences wide apart, we talk in shouts.
A constant battle of wills, moral high ground,
nobody wins in friction addiction darkest clouds.

Seduce Me!

Come thrill me! Come closer to me!
Show me love flying on wings carefree.
Your misty eyes taunt me up and down,
pink flesh skin a tale of sexy satin gown.

Breathe love talk into my open, willing ears,
allow me to shiver and quiver without any fear.
Your soft, soothing touch, so sensitive inside,
fingers exploring, imploring wild senses alive.

World outside ignored, let's live desire moments,
Immersed in our love bubble's blissful content.
A love boat floats us on a tide's sexual stream,
carrying romance a course forever so serene!

Seduction line ripples, tingles our soapy skin,
delicious excitement, shower room sexual sins.
Silky sheets tangle, wrap our bodies in ecstasy,
we lay together in timeless, endless erotic fantasy.

So Cool!

I am the latest sensation, watch me go!
fashion icon label, people in the know.
Look at me! Hair styled in tinted colours,
cold ice personality, attitude of dishonour.

I walk the streets smoking and chewing gum,
look at my mirror reflection, face white vallium.
Move out the way! I rule the roost supreme,
I'm the king around here, cat got the cream!

Slicked black hair, clothes shiny as tin foil,
Casanova ambition, ladies dirt in money soil.
So wicked, cool! Nothing can hurt or frighten me,
I'm the guy with respect, steel heart of sleaze.

Gang leader lifestyle, cronies fall to my knees,
betrayal, vendettas a wood with rope death trees.
Remember what I say goes; don't push your luck,
I don't conform to rules, society blue print sucks!

Why Black Skies?

Rising water, fear washes the land,
heaven's relentless devil anger hand.
Black skies why? Why do you cry?
Our land is awash, faith begins to die.

Nature's wrath strikes unfortunate creatures,
flooding hearts & minds a sodden damp picture.
It gushes & flows rage weight of heavy stone,
sweeps reality, hope in trails of stricken homes.

Rivers climb higher, tears fill water levels high,
time after time same situation, dark angry skies.
Rainy days never stop; relinquish its tight grip,
lives tossed, thrown like a storm stranded ship.

Hours pass slowly; fierce waters shatter dreams,
leaves people, animals no drinking water clean.
Why black skies? Why do you cry?
Let the sun dry our hopes, keep faith alive.

Mind adrift.

Senses float, glide along a mind's pathway,
trying to read signals, direction flow days.
Your face, eyes light a flame inside my soul,
nothing else matters except loving you whole.

I wander with no idea of time or direction,
lost sheep in love's smothering complication.
Time passes slowly, so slowly, never relents,
our bodies desiring an end to sexual pretence.

We are forever adrift, oceans apart it seems,
too many difficulties trip up destiny's dream.
Losing you, losing love is an inevitable outcome,
prisoners absconding, escaped on freedom run.

Naivety, insecurity overwhelmed commonsense,
love a pedestal tall, cloud high reach of innocence.
Tears well inside out, fall mercury levels design,
contemplation, reasons deep as an old coal mine.

Mind and hearts adrift, vacant journey less days,
coming together an impossible dream flown away.
We were in the hands of fate's unhappy mercy,
so far apart looking for love's lost sanctuary.

One for the Road.

A centuries old age tradition haunts us today,
public house custom of alcohol induced play.
One too many drinks, tall glasses always full,
noisy atmosphere ringing in disco music halls.

Social intercourse forsaken in foolish drunken ways,
20th century lady drinks, fights on streets of dismay.
Happy hour, clock watching, a publican's schemes,
squeeze last drop of money, a brewery's' dream!

Entertainment is vodka glasses lined table high,
competition to drink one another high and dry.
A disease eats the fabric of society's mental state,
turning kind, intelligent people into vitriolic traits.

One more for the road, they plead with friends!
Drink driver in hospital, car left road on a bend.
Where to draw the line, put conclusions in motion,
when a country is dependant on alcohol devotion.

In the frame!

I'm innocent, blameless, totally in the clear,
apportioning guilt is your way of hiding fear.
You say it's my fault, who else could it be?
I've been framed yet again, it's plain to see.

Lost man stood in life's false identity parade,
your weapon a character assassination tirade.
Bad things come in threes, so it's believed,
condemned man stood under a lightning tree.

In the frame again, how do I escape despise?
Love's fortune wheel lacks any compromise.
Experience doesn't help relieve constant pain,
It's written in black & white, answers insane.

There's no hiding place, truth is wide open,
fingers point, indicate where love is broken.
You say someone has to take certain blame,
but why is it always me in the frame?

Foolish Notion!

A social dilemma confuses the vacant mind,
tussle sensible actions, dance distorted lines.
Restless infatuation with someone out of reach,
emotions tarnish, burn caustic as bleach.

Morals, principles twisting in tales of sorrow,
will selfish thoughts decide love of tomorrow?
Permutations, conclusion of actions irresponsible,
never able to deny feelings strong, so undeniable.

Family disruption, torn between right and wrong,
destroys relationships built on foundations strong.
A flash of electricity sparking off equal minds,
guilty feelings run in dark circles hard to define.

Foolish ideas, notions heading for sobbing tears,
reluctant to stop this tidal wave awash with fear.
A heart stuck on a windmill's turning confusion,
gyrating in endless light blinding love delusion.

Like a rock tossed into muddy waters deep,
sinking, burying its face in a sea that weeps.
Your attraction, smile pulls with immense force,
will sense prevail over love sentiments off course?

Ladder Heart.

Tall ladder heart, arms far out of reach,
waits for love to walk his lonely beach.
Long twisty steps to desire's highest plain,
spiral to the top, don't leave me in vain!

Steep steps a journey completely unknown,
life's uncertainties weigh heavy marble stone.
Take a chance, climb up to an invisible tower,
ladder prince love, waiting for a rose flower.

Head lost in clouds dark, forever unforgiving,
come join me, release sad thoughts suffering.
I'm high in a loveless sky, reasons strained,
ladder contrite and tired of wallowing pain.

Stairways to heaven an illusionary dream,
eyes blinded by a bright cosmic love beam.
If you want to spark me, light fires to start?
Banish fear; climb up to meet my ladder heart.

Lessons Learned?

Browse through newspapers, colour TV guides,
programmes depict same ancestral war divides.
History's stark advice fades on decayed paper,
mankind's refusal to comprehend a new future.

Human intellect questions narrow minded ways,
lessons unheeded, shine hot ignorance dismay.
Earth's predicted collision course meteor fate,
awaits to unify us at heaven's shameful gate.

Holocaust horror stories, victim's sorry plight,
anger boils disbelief to the eye's bloody sight!
Modern day genocide cleansing happens today,
guilt and shame reek smells of rotten dismay.

Rhetoric, threats wasted on blind non-believers,
Ideas, solutions washed away in last hope river.
Lessons must be learned, secure earth's destiny,
life's mortal coil left to breathe in holy divinity.

To rewrite history, amend dark desperate times,
amalgamate; merge life's cracked distorted lines.
Can the lord ever forgive selfish human cruelty?
No understanding, compassion in a devil's liberty.

Pain remains the same.

I feel lost, trapped in a jumble of feelings,
heart on fire, hangs from a loveless ceiling.
In life fate & destiny are ruling fortune kings,
obsessions to and fro on a giant life swing!

A possibility of connections, directions to meet,
perfect person who will possess an aura sweet.
Gold Midas touch enriches those luckily serene,
I must obtain a seemingly unattainable dream.

I have lost belief in finding a colourful rainbow,
wide eyed spectrum vision, casts watery shadows.
Constant doubts ignite fires into a burning flame,
satisfaction incomplete, answers weak and tame.

Light-flashing time passes in never-ending speed,
glimmers of hope, maybe a chance to succeed.
No man is so blind, as a man hopelessly in love,
looking to the sky, searches guidance from above.

Resurrect our love; carry a cross shoulder high,
raise a heart to the sun, forgive sinful skies.
Thoughts collide apportion tired old blame,
all I know is that the pain remains the same!

Between the lines.

I have nowhere to turn, escape the obvious,
reading between the lines, you're not serious.
What can I do to change your minds outlook?
I am kind, loyal and my soul is an open book.

Love tribulations hang from the tallest tree,
problems accumulate and multiply by three.
Take me for what I am, what you really see,
scratch below the surface, try and believe!

Connections live far apart, completely astray,
live wires without a spark, surging in dismay.
Turn pages of my life's complicated manual,
reveal secrets that burn in a dust sheet annual.

Read between the lines, rescue man's disbelief,
pour passion sweet water on my body for relief.
No matter what, when or where try to calm me,
release these chains, listen to my suffering pleas!

Repetitive Days.

Count them up; lay them number face down,
24 long hours lined up with multiple frowns.
Monday to Saturday monotonous daily routine,
fools caught, tangled in life's diminished esteem.

Working clock minutes slowly ticking away,
we perform blank face robots in repetition ways.
Tunnel vision bureaucrats wildly spin red tape lies,
live 8 day week pressure cooker lack of compromise.

Try to grasp, collect money balanced on a high wire,
don't let it slip, fall into a flaming economic bonfire.
Repetitive days continually devour, eat fragile souls,
fingers gnawed to the bone, miserable stories extolled.

Why do we stand, face life's head banging wall?
Money disappears, fritters the hand in free fall.
Day after day we play, survive this cruel game,
precious time swallowed in financial blame!

Space a Premium.

Air pollution's thick smog clouds man's vision,
Intellectual ideals darken in a mind's suspicion.
Natural resources diminish, evaporate at will,
environment issues a deaf ear to loudest shrill.

Human brains short circuit ideas spark and burn,
gravy train influences, backhanders at every turn.
Reasons tossed in the air, figures put to the test,
water, gas, electric commodities rare, less & less.

Coastline erosion eats the land with no retreat,
greed, selfishness a green envy fighting defeat.
An eco-collision course for the next generations,
space vanishes in appalling money led deceptions.

A small island disappears under a political banner,
push and shove, highest bidder always the winner.
Squeezed sardines in city population crowded cans,
will time produce answers we can all understand?

Under the weather.

Inner soul turmoil blows hot and cold,
life's ups and downs, complications bold.
All around me people smile, laugh and enjoy,
Inside my heart feels tossed like a broken toy!

Rainfall plunges heavy, cold sodden tears,
I'm under the weather, lost in many fears.
I demand attention, love from you every day,
bring forth sunshine, light up withering dismay.

Time we spend, enjoy together in hours few,
your company charming, soft words so true.
I look at your face, kindness radiates wide,
I'm lucky, happy to escape places I hide.

If today or tomorrow under the weather I feel,
I will search, demand love arrives for real.
Clouds disappear, scatter when you smile,
It lifts my spirit, flies me blue sky high.

Watching Shadow.

Tall ghostly figure stares, watches over me,
white hollow face, his body blurred unseen.
Thoughts, actions once prominent disappear,
this glaring shadow smiles his constant sneer.

Life's hard lessons reflect images deranged,
obstinate, stubborn face truths denied again.
I look deep inside; a soul points its message,
take opportunities, sift through the wreckage.

Ghost shadow indicates, sends advice my way,
signs illegible, deceptive, mind games he plays.
East or west, who knows the correct direction?
Experience reminds of false hope predictions.

A free spirit always disguises the real truth,
confuses the mind, seeks undeniable proof.
If I ignore advice for too many painful years,
will I learn to conquer those nagging fears?

My ghostly shadow laughs, tells me I'm wrong,
pointing bony finger accusations, tall and long.
Watching spectre fades in misty night air,
do I accept his advice, or live without a care?

Where are you?

Anticipation time feels alive & exciting,
my questions ready, answers enlightening.
I wait nervously, palms hot & sweaty,
time passes by with increasing uncertainty.

Synchronised watches show minutes lost,
seed of love vanished, a high price & cost.
Searching for clues, you're hard to discover,
accepting my hopes, dreams are finally over.

The rain pours down in metal sheet lines,
outside a restaurant, I was surely on time!
My rain filled eyes scour the empty street,
cold night time assignation wears defeat.

Where are you? Where did you go?
My mind explodes, thoughts racing aglow.
Love vanished in thin air, severe frustration,
hope, happiness disappeared in disillusion.

Love stars collide, crumbles into moon dust,
connections broken, love metal turned to rust.
I would climb mountains, move heaven & earth,
to be together, reclaim love's chance of rebirth.

Walking Nowhere.

I walk mind disorientation along dark lanes,
conclusions awry, answers blank and plain.
Love plagues, wash spins mixed up doubts,
soul searches lost reasoning, I need to shout.

I scan narrow currents squeezing the brain,
left out in the cold, life inside fully drained.
To trace, gather senses in red paint shame,
hopes disappear among rising anxiety's blame.

Decisions confused in hot & cold water flow,
love unrequited, desired, vanished long ago.
Walking to nowhere, destination unknown,
romance diminished, last hope chances blown.

Pointless game solitaire, a comfort unreal,
It gambles with my soul, false double deal.
Reappear from somewhere, dry acid tears,
wipe away empty years full of many fears.

Love road connection far in the distance,
shine your love torch, guide me assistance.
A lonely path to follow, never looking behind,
walking out to nowhere, eyes forever blind.

Chasing Rainbows.

Colour blind race for success, constant rush,
life's too short, relax, enjoy a little sleepy hush!
You're chasing, clamouring for something rare,
pot of gold at the end of the rainbow, beware!

There's no tomorrow, you live for glory days,
pound sign eyes distract, prevent easier ways.
Time lost years fall like leaves on money trees,
It's too late for regrets, praying on bended knees.

Trace lines of success cast shadows deep,
people disregarded, promises you didn't keep.
Candle burned both ends all for material gain,
old age's dawn reveals truth washed up in vain.

Rainbow chaser, time has run its course line,
count the money, the friends, say what's fine!
Time lost reflections plague a guilty mind,
chasing an elusive rainbow you cannot find!.

Footprints in the snow.

Cold white blanket scene is painted far and wide,
landscape covered icing cake mono colour design.
Footsteps mark trace patterns of tribal civilisation life,
small indelible clues to a wilderness living barren strife.

Cold, frozen breath smoke fills long winter days,
nomadic people wander, slide into a season's dismay.
Wrapped head to toe, wear thick clothes piercing stares,
furry animal imitations shuffling around like polar bears.

Harsh unpredictable life ignored by spoiled western eyes,
walk in deep forest, collect wood in fire survival disguise.
Men & women trudge tired footsteps through deep snow,
an existence suffered in ancestral traditions lantern glow.

Mountains, valleys and rivers are their habitat homes,
money an illusion in food desperate reality igloo domes.
Life is endured, survived by a race cyclically duty bound,
content to be a secret civilisation forever lost and found!

Set Sail.

Blue ocean waves crash relationship shore,
our love boat wilderness in time unexplored.
Midday sun beats down, journey tiring and hot,
we set sail towards distant horizons passion forgot.

An abandoned ship searches hope reconciliation,
travelling emotional waters long passed destination.
Salt water overflow leaves obsession bad taste,
decisions swiftly taken, drowned in soluble haste.

Cold bitter winds freeze love into submission,
hearts shiver in a winter chill factor disposition.
We are lost, drifting, praying to be saved,
future love in the hands of a fortune wave.

We ride love's turbulent waves, stormy nights,
Ignore dangers and suspicion, sail out of sight.
Crystal pattern tides lead us to a brighter day,
searching secret love sanctuary in freedom bay.

Printed in the United States
209422BV00001B/258/P

THE
LEA
&
PERRINS
BOOK

THE
LEA
&
PERRINS
BOOK

INTRODUCTION

From a Bolognese sauce to a cheese toastie, there is very little that cannot be improved with a splash of Lea & Perrins Worcestershire Sauce. This delectable savoury sauce has been a kitchen staple for over 100 years, adding flavour to soups, stews, marinades and more. In this book, we're going to share 30 delicious recipes featuring Lea & Perrins, plus a host of fascinating facts about the history of this iconic sauce.

Find out how two chemists accidentally stumbled upon the perfect formula for a show-stopping sauce, and discover some of the unusual places historians have come across this instantly recognisable bottle. From our recipe for a scrumptious steak with brandy sauce to an amazing trip back in time to the Lea & Perrins factory, this book celebrates everyone's favourite condiment in all its glory.

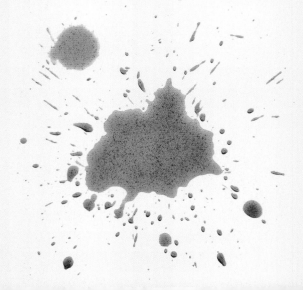

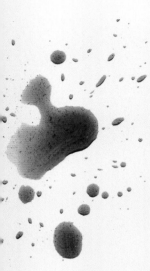

A BRIEF HISTORY OF LEA & PERRINS WORCESTERSHIRE SAUCE

I n 1835, Lord Sandys, the Governor of Bengal, returned to England and asked his local chemists – John Wheeley Lea and William Perrins – if they could try and recreate a delicious sauce he had discovered during his time abroad. They followed his recipe and concocted a batch, but were disappointed by the flavour, which was harsh and unpleasant. They stored the unappetising sauce in stone jars in their cellar, and forgot all about it.

Almost two years later, the chemists came across the jars once more and decided to give the sauce another taste. They were amazed: the ingredients had matured, and the sauce was now delicious.

With the permission of Lord Sandys, they made more, and started selling it commercially from their chemist shop on Broad Street. They also sent salesmen to docks in Southampton, Liverpool and London to sell the sauce to passenger liners to serve in their dining rooms.

By 1843, they were selling 14,500 bottles a year, and in 1897 they opened the Midland Road Factory in Worcester, where the sauce is still made today. The company merged with another iconic sauce producer, HP Sauce, in 1930, and in 2005 they became part of the Kraft Heinz group. Almost 200 years after the sauce was first created, it has become an essential ingredient in our kitchens, with 43 million bottles produced every year.

William Henry Perrins

THE LEA & PERRINS WORCESTERSHIRE SAUCE TIMELINE

Lord Sandys asks two chemists, John Wheeley Lea and William Perrins, to create a sauce using a recipe he picked up on his travels. The results are not appealing!

Lea & Perrins Worcestershire Sauce is first sold commercially.

The Lea & Perrins factory is opened on Midland Road in Worcester.

1835　**1836**　**1837**　**1850**　**1897**　**1904**

After leaving the disappointing sauce in their cellar for nearly two years, the chemists taste it again – and it is delicious.

A product licence is granted to a US company, allowing them to make Lea & Perrins Stateside.

Lea & Perrins is granted the prestigious Royal Warrant by King Edward VII.

BY APPOINTMENT
TO HER MAJESTY QUEEN ELIZABETH II
SUPPLIERS OF WORCESTERSHIRE SAUCE

Along with HP Sauce Limited, Lea & Perrins is bought by Kraft Heinz, taking its place in the kitchen cupboard of fame alongside other iconic sauces and treats.

Lea & Perrins merge with HP Sauce Ltd.

1906

1930

1988

2005

TODAY

Lea & Perrins is granted a High Court Justice ruling, allowing them to print their labels with 'Original and Genuine', thanks to all the attempted imitators trying to create their own versions of the sauce.

The group becomes part of BSN Groupe, whose name then changed to Danone in 1995.

BLOODY MARY

PREP 5 MINUTES

200ml vodka
1 litre tomato juice
2 tbsp Lea & Perrins
    Worcestershire Sauce
1 tsp crushed black pepper
zest and juice and 1 lemon
½ tsp celery salt (optional)
2–4 tsp hot sauce, depending
    on how spicy you like it
    (we like sriracha)
salt, if needed
4 celery stalks
large handful of ice

In a large jug, stir together the vodka, tomato juice, Lea & Perrins, black pepper, lemon zest and juice and celery salt (if using). Add 2 teaspoons of the hot sauce and season to taste, adding more hot sauce if you like it spicy.

To serve, fill four tall glasses with ice cubes and stick a celery stalk into each one. Pour in the Bloody Mary mix and enjoy.

The Bloody Mary mix can be made up to 4 hours in advance and kept in the fridge in the jug until you're ready to serve.

CREAMY BAKED EGGS

PREP 5 MINUTES
COOK 15 MINUTES

8 medium free-range eggs
4 tsp Lea & Perrins
   Worcestershire Sauce
small handful of chives,
   snipped
150ml double cream
salt and pepper
30g Parmesan, finely grated
400g asparagus tips
1 tbsp olive oil

Preheat the oven to 180°C/160°C fan/gas mark 4.

Crack two eggs each into four large ramekins or small baking dishes. Top each dish with 1 teaspoon of Lea & Perrins, a quarter of the chives and a quarter of the double cream. Season with lots of black pepper, then scatter over the Parmesan. Place the ramekins in a roasting tin.

Toss the asparagus tips in the olive oil on a baking tray. Season with salt and pepper, then spread out into a single layer so that they roast evenly.

Bake the eggs and asparagus for 12–15 minutes until the asparagus is tender and the eggs are just cooked with a jammy yolk centre. Serve together and enjoy.

THE LEA & PERRINS WORCESTERSHIRE SAUCE BOTTLE

The instantly recognisable Lea & Perrins bottle is characterised by its long, slim neck, which was designed to allow enough space for the sauce to be shaken in order to disperse the slight sediment that can settle at the bottom due to its long maturation process.

The label has changed a little over the years – early versions were wrapped in paper, as we see here – but the bold orange label we all know and love has stayed much the same for decades.

ORIGINAL & GENUINE

TOAD-IN-THE-HOLE

PREP 10 MINUTES
COOK 35 MINUTES

3 tbsp vegetable oil
8 good-quality pork sausages
2 red onions, each cut into
    6 wedges
salt and pepper
buttered peas, Heinz Tomato
    Ketchup and/or gravy,
    to serve (optional)

For the Yorkshire pudding
    batter
4 medium free-range eggs
125g self-raising flour
300ml whole milk
2 tbsp Lea & Perrins
    Worcestershire Sauce

Preheat the oven to 220°C/200°C fan/gas mark 7.

Begin by mixing the Yorkshire pudding batter. Crack the eggs into a large bowl. Add the flour, milk and Lea & Perrins, then whisk well until a smooth batter forms. Pour this into a large jug and set aside.

Pour the oil into a medium-sized roasting tin. Add the sausages and red onion wedges, and season with salt and pepper. Roast for 10 minutes until the sausages begin to brown.

Remove the tin from the oven, then quickly and carefully pour in the batter. Return to the oven for 20–25 minutes until the Yorkshire pudding is puffed up and a deep golden brown. Don't be tempted to open the oven door before the timer goes off, as this may deflate the Yorkshire.

Serve the toad-in-the-hole at the table for everyone to help themselves. We like to serve this with buttered peas, ketchup and gravy.

COLCANNON

PREP 10 MINUTES
COOK 30 MINUTES

1kg floury potatoes (we
    like Maris Piper or King
    Edwards), peeled and
    halved
salt and pepper
60g salted butter
12 streaky bacon rashers,
    chopped
1 small savoy cabbage, finely
    sliced
3 garlic cloves, finely chopped
150ml double cream
2 tsp Lea & Perrins
    Worcestershire Sauce

Put the potatoes into a large saucepan of cold salted water. Bring to the boil, then cook for around 20 minutes until completely tender; a cutlery knife should slide into the centre of a potato with no resistance.

Meanwhile, melt 10g of the butter in a large frying pan over a medium–high heat. Add the bacon and fry, stirring regularly, for 5 minutes until crisp. Add the garlic to the pan and cook, still stirring, for 30 seconds more, then tip in the cabbage.

Pour 50ml water into the frying pan. Cook the cabbage, stirring occasionally, for 8–10 minutes until softened and collapsed, then take the pan off the heat.

Drain the cooked potatoes into a colander and leave to steam dry for a few minutes, then tip them back into the saucepan. Add the remaining 50g of butter, then mash well using a potato masher. Beat in the double cream and Lea & Perrins until smooth, then tip the mash into the frying pan with the bacon and cabbage.

Give everything a good mix to combine and season to taste.

This would be delicious served with the Meatloaf opposite.

MEATLOAF

PREP 10 MINUTES
COOK 50 MINUTES

1 tsp olive oil, for greasing
1kg good-quality beef mince
2 onions, halved and grated
4 fat garlic cloves, crushed
2 medium free-range eggs
2 tbsp Lea & Perrins
  Worcestershire Sauce
1 tbsp Dijon mustard
1 tbsp Italian dried herbs
100g panko breadcrumbs
salt and pepper
4 tbsp Heinz Tomato Ketchup
1 tbsp apple cider vinegar
1 tbsp soft light brown sugar

Preheat the oven to 180°C/160°C fan/gas mark 4. Grease the inside of a 900g loaf tin with the oil.

Tip the beef mince into a large bowl, along with the grated onions and crushed garlic. Crack in the eggs, then add the Lea & Perrins, mustard, dried herbs and breadcrumbs, along with plenty of salt and pepper.

Using clean hands, knead everything into the meat so that it is evenly distributed, then form the mixture into a rough oblong the size of your loaf tin. Place it inside the tin.

Stir the ketchup, vinegar and brown sugar together in a small bowl until the sugar dissolves, then brush the mixture all over the top and any exposed sides of the meatloaf.

Roast for 45–50 minutes until juicy and cooked through. Leave to cool for 5 minutes before slicing.

We like to eat this with the Colcannon opposite.

WHAT'S IN LEA & PERRINS?

The precise recipe for Lea & Perrins Worcestershire Sauce
is top-secret; from the very beginning, Mr Lea and
Mr Perrins knew they were on to something very special,
and they took care to keep their formula secret. Even
today, **only nine people** know exactly how it's
made.

What we can share, though, are some of the key
ingredients: shallots, garlic, vinegar, chillies
– and **anchovies!**

It's a very slow process that takes about three years from beginning to end. The various ingredients are matured individually in vinegar or salt for differing amounts of time before being combined to make the sauce, which is then bottled. It's not just the exact blend of ingredients that's important, but also how long each one is matured for. Every step of the process is vital to create the most delicious sauce possible.

The classic
Bloody Mary
cocktail was created in Harry's New York Bar in Paris in 1921. Bartender Fernand Petiot added a splash of Lea & Perrins to tomato juice and vodka, and the rest is history. See our version on page 12.

Lieutenant Colonel Younghusband, the first European visitor to the forbidden city of Lhasa in Tibet, was impressed when he arrived in 1904 and discovered that a bottle of Lea & Perrins had made it there before he did.

In 1886, the city of Te Wairoa in New Zealand was destroyed by a volcano. When excavations took place almost 100 years later in the 1970s, historians unearthed an undamaged bottle of Lea & Perrins, which had been there since before the eruption.

For those with fancy dining rooms, elaborate silver covers were specially designed to adorn Lea & Perrins bottles so they looked elegant on the table.

LEEK & GOAT'S CHEESE QUICHE

PREP 10 MINUTES, PLUS 20 MINUTES CHILLING
COOK 1 HOUR 10 MINUTES

500g block shortcrust pastry
plain flour, for dusting
50g salted butter
3 leeks, halved and finely
   sliced
salt and pepper
handful of thyme, leaves
   stripped
zest of 1 lemon
3 garlic cloves, crushed
3 medium free-range eggs
100ml whole milk
150ml double cream
1 tbsp Lea & Perrins
   Worcestershire Sauce
75g goat's cheese
salad, to serve

You will need baking beans or
raw rice.

Roll out the pastry on a lightly floured work surface to a thickness of 5mm, then use it to line a 22cm tart tin. Lightly press around the edges and trim any excess pastry. Prick the base of the pastry with a fork, then chill for 20 minutes.

Meanwhile, preheat the oven to 200°C/180°C fan/gas mark 6. Melt the butter in a large frying pan over a medium heat. Add the leeks, along with a pinch of salt, and cook, stirring occasionally, for 8–10 minutes until softened. Add most of the thyme and all the lemon zest. Add the garlic and cook for 30 seconds more, then remove the pan from the heat.

Place a large sheet of baking paper over the chilled pastry. Fill with baking beans or rice, then blind-bake for 15 minutes until the sides of the pastry are set and lightly golden.

Meanwhile, crack the eggs into a jug. Add the milk, cream and Lea & Perrins. Season and whisk well.

Remove the paper and beans or rice from the pastry case, then return it to the oven for 5 minutes until the base is cooked. Reduce the oven temperature to 160°C/140°F/gas mark 3. Spread the leeks across the bottom of the pastry case, then pour over the cream mixture. Dot over the goat's cheese and remaining thyme, then return the tart to the oven. Bake for 30–40 minutes until the quiche has just set and is lightly golden. Leave to cool for at least 10–15 minutes before slicing. Serve warm or cold with a big salad.

SHEPHERD'S PIE

PREP 10 MINUTES
COOK 1¼ HOURS

2 tbsp olive oil
500g good-quality lamb mince
1 large onion, finely chopped
salt and pepper
3 carrots, peeled and diced
small handful of rosemary,
    leaves picked and finely
    chopped
2 tbsp tomato purée
1 tbsp plain flour
500ml beef stock
1 tbsp + 2 tsp Lea & Perrins
    Worcestershire Sauce
750g floury potatoes (we
    like Maris Piper or King
    Edwards), peeled and
    halved
75g salted butter
300g frozen peas
50g extra-mature Cheddar,
    grated

Heat 1 tablespoon of the oil in a large frying pan over a high heat. Season the lamb with salt and pepper, then add half to the pan. Fry for 6–8 minutes, stirring and breaking it down, until crisp and browned. Remove with a slotted spoon into a bowl and repeat with the remaining mince.

Once all the mince is fried and in the bowl, heat the remaining 1 tablespoon of oil in the empty pan. Add the onion and carrots and reduce the heat to medium. Cook for 8–10 minutes, stirring occasionally, until softened. Return the lamb to the pan and stir in the rosemary and tomato purée. Cook for 1 minute more, then add the flour. Cook, stirring, for another minute, then pour in the beef stock. Add 1 tablespoon of the Lea & Perrins, then leave to bubble away while you make the mash.

Put the potatoes into a saucepan of cold salted water. Bring to the boil, then cook for 20 minutes until completely tender. Drain into a colander and steam dry for a few minutes, then tip back into the saucepan. Add the butter and the remaining 2 teaspoons of Lea & Perrins, along with plenty of salt and pepper, and mash using a potato masher.

Stir the peas into the lamb mixture and season to taste, then spoon into a medium-sized baking dish. Spread the mash on top, then scatter over the grated cheese. Bake for 20 minutes until the pie is bubbling and the top is golden brown. Leave to cool for 5 minutes before serving.

LANCASHIRE HOTPOT

PREP 15 MINUTES
COOK 2½ HOURS

800g good-quality lamb neck
    fillet, cut into medium-sized
    chunks
salt and pepper
2 tbsp olive oil
2 large onions, sliced
2 tbsp plain flour
600ml chicken stock
1 tbsp Lea & Perrins
    Worcestershire Sauce
250g baby carrots (we like
    Chantenay), kept whole
    and unpeeled
4 bay leaves
small handful of thyme sprigs
800g floury potatoes (we
    like Maris Piper or King
    Edwards), peeled and
    finely sliced
50g salted butter, melted
buttery greens, to serve
    (optional)

You will need a pastry brush

Preheat the oven to 160°C/140°F/gas mark 3.

Season the lamb chunks with salt and pepper. Heat the oil in a large frying pan over a medium–high heat. Working in batches, fry the lamb chunks for around 2 minutes on each side until nicely browned. Transfer to a casserole pot. Repeat until all the lamb is browned and in the casserole pot.

Reduce the heat to medium and add the onions to the frying pan, along with a pinch of salt. Cook, stirring occasionally, for 8–10 minutes until softened but not coloured. Add the flour and cook, stirring, for 1 minute more, then add the chicken stock. Keep stirring until well combined, then add the Lea & Perrins, carrots, bay and thyme. Give everything a good mix and season well with salt and pepper, then pour this mixture over the lamb in the casserole pot.

Arrange the potato slices in an overlapping pattern over the top of the lamb, brushing them regularly with the melted butter and seasoning with salt and pepper.

Cover with a lid and cook in the oven for 1½ hours. Remove the lid and cook, uncovered, for an additional 30 minutes. For extra colour on the potatoes, you can slide the hotpot under the grill for the final few minutes of cooking.

Leave to cool for 5 minutes before serving. Serve with buttery greens, if you like.

CAULIFLOWER CHEESE

PREP 10 MINUTES
COOK 35 MINUTES

2 medium-sized cauliflowers,
   outer leaves removed, each
   cut into 6 wedges
3 tbsp olive oil
salt and pepper
60g salted butter
60g plain flour
750ml whole milk
200g Gruyère, coarsely grated
1 tbsp + 1 tsp Lea & Perrins
   Worcestershire Sauce
2 garlic cloves, crushed
50g panko breadcrumbs

Preheat the oven to 200°C/180°C fan/gas mark 6.

Lay the cauliflower wedges, cut-side up, in a medium-sized roasting tin. It's OK if they fit a little snugly; they will shrink as they roast. Drizzle over 2 tablespoons of the oil and season with salt and pepper. Roast for 15 minutes.

Meanwhile, melt the butter in a large saucepan over a medium heat. Once melted, whisk in the flour. Cook, whisking, for 2 minutes, then, still whisking continuously, pour in the milk, a little at a time, waiting for each addition to become smoothly incorporated into the flour before adding more.

Once all the milk has been added, let the sauce bubble away for 5 minutes, whisking occasionally, until thick and smooth. Stir in 150g of the cheese and 1 tablespoon of the Lea & Perrins, then season to taste and take off the heat.

In a small bowl, mix together the garlic and breadcrumbs. Stir in the remaining 1 tablespoon of oil, along with the 1 teaspoon of Lea & Perrins and the rest of the cheese. Stir to combine.

Remove the roasting tin from the oven and pour the cheese sauce over the roasted cauliflower wedges. Scatter over the cheesy breadcrumbs, then return to the oven for 20 minutes until bubbling and golden. Leave to cool for 5 minutes before tucking in.

ULTIMATE LASAGNE

PREP 15 MINUTES
COOK 4 HOURS

1kg good-quality diced beef shin
salt and pepper
3 tbsp olive oil
1 large onion, chopped
4 fat garlic cloves, crushed
250ml red wine
2 x 400g tins plum tomatoes
4 bay leaves
2 tsp caster sugar
2 tbsp Lea & Perrins Worcestershire Sauce
50g salted butter
50g plain flour
700ml whole milk
½ nutmeg, grated
500g dried lasagne sheets
50g Parmesan, finely grated

Season the beef well with salt and pepper. Heat 2 tablespoons of the olive oil in your largest saucepan over a high heat. Working in batches, fry the beef for around 2 minutes on each side until nicely browned. Transfer to a bowl using a slotted spoon. Repeat until all the beef is browned and in the bowl.

Pour the remaining 1 tablespoon of oil into the pan and reduce the heat to medium. Add the onion, along with a pinch of salt. Cook, stirring occasionally, for 8–10 minutes until softened but not coloured. Add the garlic and cook for 30 seconds more, then add the red wine and plum tomatoes. Return the beef to the pan, along with the bay leaves, sugar and 1 tablespoon of the Lea & Perrins. Stir, then reduce the heat to low. Cover and simmer, stirring now and then, for 3 hours until the beef is meltingly tender. Shred the beef into the sauce and season.

Preheat the oven to 200°C/180°C fan/gas mark 6. Melt the butter in a saucepan over a medium heat. Add the flour and cook, whisking, for 2 minutes, then, still whisking, gradually pour in the milk, letting each addition become smoothly incorporated before adding more. Once all the milk has been added, let the sauce bubble away, whisking occasionally, for 5 minutes until smooth and thick. Stir in the nutmeg, and the remaining 1 tablespoon of Lea & Perrins. Season to taste and take off the heat.

To assemble the lasagne, spread a little of the white sauce across the bottom of a deep 30 x 20cm baking dish, then cover with a layer of lasagne sheets. Top with a thick layer of ragu, followed by some more white sauce and then more lasagne sheets. Repeat until all the ragu and lasagne sheets have been used up, finishing with a layer of white sauce.

Scatter over the grated Parmesan, then bake for 45–50 minutes until the pasta is cooked through and the lasagne is bubbling and golden brown. Leave to cool for 10 minutes before serving.

CROQUE MADAME

PREP 5 MINUTES
COOK 45 MINUTES

25g salted butter
25g plain flour
250ml whole milk
2 tsp Lea & Perrins
   Worcestershire Sauce, plus
   a splash to serve
salt and pepper
4 thick slices of brioche or
   white bread
2 tsp Dijon mustard
100g Gruyère, grated
4 thick slices of good-quality
   ham
1 tbsp olive oil
2 medium free-range eggs
chicory salad, to serve
   (optional)

Preheat the oven to 180°C/160°C fan/gas mark 4. Line a roasting tray with baking paper.

Melt the butter in a saucepan over a medium heat. Add the flour and cook, whisking, for 2 minutes, then, still whisking, gradually pour in the milk, letting each addition become smoothly incorporated before adding more. Once all the milk has been added, let the sauce bubble away, whisking occasionally, for 5 minutes until smooth and thick. Add the Lea & Perrins and season to taste, then remove from the heat. Leave to cool for 10 minutes.

Place two slices of the bread on the prepared roasting tray. Spread each slice with 1 teaspoon of the mustard, followed by a quarter of the cooled white sauce. Divide most of the Gruyère between them, followed by the ham. Sandwich together with the remaining bread. Spread the remaining white sauce over the top of the sandwiches and scatter over the remaining cheese. Carefully transfer the tray containing the sandwiches to the oven and bake for 12–15 minutes until the cheese has melted and the sandwiches are golden brown.

Once the sandwiches are nearly cooked, heat the oil in a small frying pan over a high heat. Crack in the eggs and fry for 2–3 minutes until cooked to your liking.

Put the sandwiches on to two plates. Top each one with a fried egg and a good splash of Lea & Perrins. Serve with a chicory salad, if you like.

THE LEA & PERRINS FACTORY

The Lea & Perrins factory was opened
on Midland Road in Worcester in 1897.

The ingredients were matured in huge barrels in the cellar until they were ready to be mixed together to create the sauce.

The sauce was then bottled and prepared for packaging...

...before being shipped out to shops and consumers.

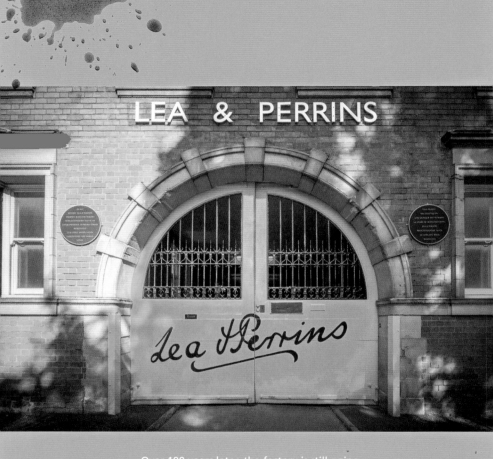

Over 100 years later, the factory is still going,
and the sauce is made in the same way…

...starting with barrels in the cellar and ending up in your kitchen.

After all, why would you mess with perfection?

FRENCH ONION SOUP

SERVES 4

PREP 10 MINUTES
COOK 1 HOUR

6 onions, finely sliced
2 tbsp olive oil
salt and pepper
2 tbsp soft light brown sugar
2 tbsp Lea & Perrins
  Worcestershire Sauce, plus
  a dash to serve
250ml white wine or brandy
1.3 litres chicken or beef stock
8 thick slices of bread (we like
  ciabatta, cob or sourdough)
50g softened salted butter
150g Comté, grated

Put the onions into your largest saucepan over a medium heat. Pour in 400ml water and cook for 20 minutes or so, until all the water has evaporated and the onions have collapsed. Increase the heat to medium–high, then add the olive oil and a good pinch of salt. Fry, stirring regularly, for 10 minutes, until the onions are beginning to caramelise, then stir through the brown sugar and Lea & Perrins. Cook for a further 5 minutes until sticky and golden brown.

Pour in the white wine or brandy and allow to bubble away until the liquid volume has reduced by half. Now pour in the stock and give everything a good stir, then leave the soup to simmer away while you make the toasts.

Preheat the grill to high. Lay the bread slices on a roasting tray and grill for 1 minute on each side until lightly toasted.

Spread the butter over the toasts, then divide the grated cheese between each slice. Slide back under the grill for 2–3 minutes until the cheese is melted and the toasts are bubbling and golden brown.

Season the soup to taste and serve with the cheese toasts.

The soup can happily be made up to 2 days in advance and kept, covered, in the fridge.

CAESAR SALAD

PREP 5 MINUTES
COOK 40 MINUTES

6 skin-on, bone-in chicken
   thighs
salt and pepper
3 tbsp olive oil
3 slices of white crusty bread,
   cut into large croutons
   (we like ciabatta, cob or
   sourdough)
2 romaine lettuces, leaves
   roughly sliced
zest of 1 lemon
30g Parmesan, shaved

For the dressing
50ml olive oil
2 medium free-range egg
   yolks
1 garlic clove, peeled
2 tsp Dijon mustard
4 anchovies in oil (optional)
**2 tsp Lea & Perrins
   Worcestershire Sauce**
juice of 1 lemon
20g Parmesan, finely grated

Preheat the oven to 200°C/180°C fan/gas mark 6.

Season the chicken thighs all over with salt and pepper. Lay on a large roasting tray, skin-side up, and drizzle over 2 tablespoons of the olive oil. Roast for 30 minutes.

Meanwhile, make the dressing. Place all the dressing ingredients into a powerful blender and blitz until a smooth, creamy dressing is formed. You may need to add 1–2 tablespoons of water if the dressing is a little thick. Season to taste – we like this with lots of black pepper – then set aside.

After the chicken has been roasting for 30 minutes, remove from the oven and add the croutons to the roasting tray with the chicken. Pour over the remaining 1 tablespoon of olive oil and season the bread well with salt and pepper. Return to the oven for 10 minutes until the chicken is cooked through and the croutons are crisp.

Slice the roasted chicken meat away from the bone.

Toss the lettuce, chicken, croutons and dressing together in a large salad bowl. Top with the lemon zest and Parmesan shavings to serve.

You can make the dressing a few hours in advance and keep in the fridge. It will thicken slightly once chilled, so stir in a splash of warm water to loosen before using.

CHEESY POTATO SKINS

PREP 10 MINUTES
COOK 1¼ HOURS

4 baking potatoes (we like
  King Edwards), scrubbed
salt and pepper
1 tbsp olive oil
1 fat garlic clove, crushed
180g cream cheese
handful of parsley, roughly
  chopped (stalks and all)
2 tbsp Lea & Perrins
  Worcestershire Sauce
½ tsp smoked paprika, plus
  extra to serve
100g extra-mature Cheddar,
  grated

Preheat the oven to 200°C/180°C fan/gas mark 6.

Prick the potatoes all over with a sharp knife. Put on a roasting tray and sprinkle with salt and black pepper. Bake for 1 hour until cooked through.

Once the potatoes are cooked, leave to cool slightly. Increase the oven temperature to 220°C/200°C fan/gas mark 7.

Cut the cooled potatoes in half. Scoop the soft middles into a large bowl and put the skins back on the roasting tray. Drizzle the skins with the oil and season with a little more salt and pepper, then return to the oven for 5 minutes to crisp up.

Meanwhile, stir the garlic into the cooked potato filling, along with the cream cheese, parsley, Lea & Perrins, smoked paprika and most of the Cheddar. Mix well to combine and season to taste.

Stuff the potato filling back into the crisped-up skins, then scatter over the remaining cheese. Bake in the oven for a further 8–12 minutes until the cheese is melted and they are bubbling and golden. Sprinkle with a little smoked paprika to serve.

SALMON COBB SALAD

PREP 10 MINUTES
COOK 6½ MINUTES

salt and pepper
2 medium free-range eggs
zest and juice of 1 lemon
1 avocado, peeled, stoned
  and sliced
1 tbsp balsamic vinegar
3 tbsp olive oil
1 tsp Lea & Perrins
  Worcestershire Sauce
100g cherry tomatoes on the
  vine, picked and halved
1 romaine lettuce, sliced
200g sustainably sourced hot
  smoked or poached salmon,
  flaked into large pieces
50g feta, crumbled

Bring a small saucepan of salted water to the boil. Drop in the eggs and cook for 6½ minutes (set a timer).

Meanwhile, squeeze half the lemon juice over the sliced avocado to keep it from going brown.

In a large bowl, mix together the balsamic, olive oil, Lea & Perrins, lemon zest and remaining lemon juice. Season the dressing to taste, then add the tomatoes and toss to coat.

Once the eggs are cooked, drain into a sieve and rinse under cold water until cool enough to handle, then peel and halve.

Add the lettuce to the bowl with the tomatoes and dressing. Toss to combine, then divide between two plates. Top with the avocado, salmon, feta and jammy soft-boiled egg to serve.

CHEAT'S
PISSALADIÈRE TART

PREP 15 MINUTES
COOK 20 MINUTES

200g caramelised onion
chutney

1 tbsp Lea & Perrins
Worcestershire Sauce

320g ready-rolled puff pastry

18 anchovies in oil

100g pitted black olives,
halved

small handful of thyme, leaves
picked

tomato and rocket salad,
to serve (optional)

You will need a pastry brush

Preheat the oven to 200°C/180°C fan/gas mark 6.

In a small bowl, mix together the caramelised onion chutney and Lea & Perrins. Unravel the sheet of puff pastry, then spread the chutney mixture across the pastry sheet, leaving a 1cm border around the edges.

Lay the anchovies in a criss-cross pattern on top, then dot over the olives and scatter over the thyme leaves. Brush the pastry borders with the anchovy oil, then bake for 20 minutes. The pastry should be puffed up and deeply golden.

Leave to cool for a few minutes before cutting into four or five pieces. We like to serve this with a tomato and rocket salad.

LEA & PERRINS LAMB LEG

PREP 15 MINUTES
COOK 1½ HOURS

2kg whole leg of lamb
salt and pepper
1.5kg new potatoes, halved
3 fennel bulbs, quartered
    lengthways
3 tbsp olive oil
2 tsp fennel seeds
1 tsp dried chilli flakes
    (optional)
400g cherry tomatoes on the
    vine
1 garlic bulb, bulb halved
    through the equator and
    cloves peeled
green salad and Salsa Verde
    (opposite), to serve
    (optional)

For the marinade
2 fat garlic cloves, crushed
2 tbsp Lea & Perrins
    Worcestershire Sauce
2 tbsp olive oil
handful of rosemary, leaves
    picked and chopped

Remove the lamb from the fridge an hour before you begin cooking. Preheat the oven to 200°C/180°C fan/gas mark 6.

For the marinade, combine the crushed garlic, Lea & Perrins and olive oil in a small bowl. Add half the rosemary and stir to combine. Using a sharp knife, make small incisions all over the lamb. Season with salt and pepper, then rub in the marinade.

Put the potatoes and fennel bulbs into a large roasting tin. Toss with the oil, fennel seeds, chilli flakes (if using) and plenty of salt and pepper, then spread out into an even layer. Place the roasting tin on the oven on the bottom shelf, then place the lamb on the oven bars directly over the top. Roast for 1 hour.

Remove the potatoes and fennel from the oven and toss well, then add the tomatoes, garlic and remaining rosemary. Return to the oven.

Continue roasting the lamb for a further 15–30 minutes, depending on how pink you like it, then transfer to a chopping board. Cover in foil and leave to rest for 15 minutes. Leave the vegetables in the oven to continue cooking.

When everything is ready, carve the lamb, smoosh the garlic into the fennel and potatoes, then serve with a green salad and salsa verde on the side.

SALSA VERDE

PREP 5 MINUTES

1 fat garlic clove, crushed

1 tbsp Dijon mustard

1 tbsp Lea & Perrins
    Worcestershire Sauce

6 tbsp olive oil

3 tbsp capers, drained and
    roughly chopped

100g parsley, finely chopped
    (stalks and all)

3–4 tbsp red wine vinegar

salt and pepper

In a small bowl, combine the garlic, mustard, Lea & Perrins, olive oil, capers and parsley. Add 3 tablespoons of the vinegar and stir together until well combined. Season the sauce to taste, adding more vinegar if you like a bit more of a tang.

We love serving this with all kinds of meat, especially the Lea & Perrins Lamb Leg opposite. The salsa verde will keep, covered, in the fridge for up to 3 days.

You can also make salsa verde with a mixture of soft herbs. We like basil, dill and even a bit of tarragon, so feel free to play around with the flavours as you please. It's a great way to use up herbs that are on the turn.

GOLD RUSH

In the **1840s**, Lea & Perrins
Worcestershire Sauce found itself on the
Gold Rush wagon trains. It was popular
with settlers who used it as a marinade to
tenderise buffalo and bison meat.

In **1849**, a ship sailing up the Pacific
Coast was deserted by its crew, who left
to join the Gold Rush, leaving behind their
captain and the cargo officer. Listed among
the cargo were various types of medicine –
and plenty of Lea & Perrins.

Almost two centuries later, empty Lea &
Perrins bottles discovered at archaeological
sites in Canada and the US have helped
historians identify when certain frontier
settlements were established.

MOULES MARINIÈRE

PREP 5 MINUTES
COOK 15 MINUTES

1kg live mussels in their shells
30g salted butter
2 banana shallots, finely
    chopped
salt
2 garlic cloves, crushed
250ml white wine
150ml double cream
2 tsp Lea & Perrins
    Worcestershire Sauce
handful of parsley, roughly
    chopped (stalks and all)
crusty baguette, to serve

Clean the mussels in a large bowl of cold water. Pull off any beards (the straggly threads of brown seaweed) and discard any mussels that stay open after being held shut in the palm of your hand. Drain away the water and set the cleaned mussels aside in the fridge.

Melt the butter in a large saucepan over a medium heat. Add the shallots, along with a pinch of salt. Cook, stirring occasionally, for 8–10 minutes until softened but not coloured. Add the garlic and cook for 30 seconds more.

Pour in the white wine and increase the heat to high. Bring to the boil, then tip in the mussels. Immediately cover the pan with a lid and cook, shaking the pan occasionally, for 2–3 minutes until the mussels are cooked – you will be able to tell they are ready, as their shells will have opened.

Reduce the heat to medium and add the double cream, Lea & Perrins and parsley. Stir to coat the mussels in the sauce. Simmer for 1 minute more, looking through the mussels and discarding any that remain closed.

Place the pan in the middle of the table on a heatproof mat to serve, with a crusty baguette for dunking.

WILD MUSHROOM RISOTTO

PREP 10 MINUTES
COOK 50 MINUTES

30g dried porcini mushrooms
2 tbsp Lea & Perrins
  Worcestershire Sauce
1.5 litres hot chicken stock
75g salted butter
1 tbsp olive oil
500g mixed mushrooms, sliced
  (we like a combination of
  wild, chestnut and oyster)
salt and pepper
4 fat garlic cloves, finely
  chopped
300g arborio rice
250ml white wine
50g Parmesan, finely grated
handful of tarragon or
  parsley, leaves picked and
  roughly chopped

Mix the dried porcini mushrooms and Lea & Perrins into the hot chicken stock. Set aside while you fry the mushrooms.

Melt the butter with the olive oil in a large, high-sided frying pan over a high heat. Add the mushrooms, along with a good pinch of salt. Fry, stirring regularly, for 10 minutes until deeply golden brown and crisp.

Reduce the heat to medium, then add the garlic. Cook, stirring, for 1 minute, then tip in the rice. Stir so that each grain of rice gets coated in the garlicky mushrooms, and toast in the pan for 1 minute.

Pour in the white wine. Once it has been absorbed by the rice, add a ladleful of the mushroomy chicken stock (don't worry about pieces of porcini going into the pan at the same time). Cook, stirring regularly, until this stock has been absorbed, then repeat. Keep adding the stock and mushrooms, until most of the stock has been absorbed and the rice is tender with a slight bite – this will take around 20 minutes.

Stir in most of the Parmesan, along with most of the tarragon or parsley, then season the risotto to taste.

Spoon the risotto into four bowls, and top with the remaining Parmesan and herbs to serve.

LEA & PERRINS ADVERTS THROUGH THE YEARS

The best HOT POT I ever made was prepared this way

Within the reach of everybody
9d.
1/2
and
2/-
per bottle

I removed nearly all the fat from about two pounds of the best end of neck of mutton, and then cut it into chops. These I dipped in seasoned flour and laid in the bottom of a deep dish.

Finely sliced onions and potatoes, and some sliced beef kidney were then added—and then more chops, and so on until the dish was filled. Next I added half a pint of gravy, a tablespoonful of Lea & Perrins' Sauce, and pepper and salt.

The top I covered with raw potatoes cut in halves and then let the pot—covered, of course—cook gently for two hours in a steady oven.

Lea & Perrins' Sauce
THE ORIGINAL WORCESTERSHIRE

LEA & PERRINS' SAUCE
THE ORIGINAL
"WORCESTERSHIRE"

THAT'S IT.

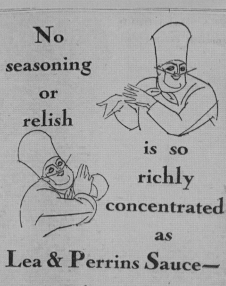

No seasoning or relish is so richly concentrated as **Lea & Perrins Sauce—** now only **1/-** a bottle!

SOLD BY ALL GOOD GROCERS
1/- A BOTTLE, <u>DOUBLE</u> SIZE 1/9

LEA & PERRINS SAUCE

By Appointment

By Appointment

LEA & PERRINS'
SAUCE

ADDS ZEST
TO FOOD

STEAK WITH BRANDY SAUCE

PREP 5 MINUTES
COOK 10 MINUTES

4 good-quality sirloin or rump
    steaks (about 225g each)
2 tbsp olive oil
salt and pepper
30g salted butter
2 banana shallots, finely
    chopped
150g chestnut mushrooms,
    sliced
2 fat garlic cloves, crushed
100ml brandy
2 tsp Dijon mustard
2 tbsp Lea & Perrins
    Worcestershire Sauce
300ml double cream
large handful of parsley, finely
    chopped (stalks and all)

Remove the steaks from the fridge 30 minutes before you begin cooking to allow them to come up to room temperature.

Rub the steaks with the oil and season generously on both sides with salt and pepper.

Heat a large non-stick frying pan over a high heat until searingly hot, then lay in the steaks. Fry to your liking (2 minutes on each side for medium-rare). Once cooked, transfer the steaks to a plate and leave to rest while you make the sauce.

Return the empty pan to a high heat (no need to wash it – we want all that extra flavour!). Add the butter and, once it has melted, add the shallots and mushrooms. Fry, stirring, for 5 minutes until soft and golden. Add the garlic and cook for 30 seconds more, then carefully pour in the brandy. It may flame a little – don't worry, this is normal!

Once the brandy is no longer alight, reduce the heat to medium and stir in the mustard, Lea & Perrins and double cream. Let the sauce bubble away for a minute or so, then remove from the heat. Stir in the parsley and season to taste.

Serve the sauce over the steaks. We like to eat this with our Dauphinoise opposite.

DAUPHINOISE

PREP 15 MINUTES
COOK 1½ HOURS

300ml double cream
300ml whole milk
2 tbsp Lea & Perrins
   Worcestershire Sauce
20g softened salted butter
1kg floury potatoes (we
   like Maris Piper or King
   Edwards), peeled and
   finely sliced
salt and pepper
3 fat garlic cloves, finely
   chopped
50g Pecorino or Parmesan,
   finely grated

Preheat the oven to 180°C/160°C fan/gas mark 4.

In a large jug, whisk together the double cream, milk and Lea & Perrins.

Dot the butter all over the bottom of a medium-sized rectangular roasting dish. Arrange the potato slices in the dish in layers, overlapping them slightly, and seasoning with salt, pepper and a scattering of chopped garlic as you go.

Once all the potatoes are layered in the dish, pour over the cream mixture. Using clean hands, press down on the potatoes to make sure they are completely submerged, then scatter over the Pecorino or Parmesan.

Tightly cover the dish in foil. Bake for 1 hour, then remove the foil and continue baking for 20–30 minutes until the potatoes are bubbling, golden brown and completely soft. A cutlery knife should slide into the centre with no resistance.

We like to serve this with the Steak with Brandy Sauce opposite for an impressive meal.

For evenly sliced potatoes, you can use a mandolin on a 5mm thickness setting.

CHEAT'S CHICKEN CHOW MEIN

PREP 5 MINUTES
COOK 10 MINUTES

2 tsp cornflour

100ml chicken stock

2 garlic cloves, crushed

1 tbsp soy sauce

1 tbsp Lea & Perrins Worcestershire Sauce

3 tbsp oyster sauce

2 tbsp sesame oil

salt and pepper

2 free-range skinless, boneless chicken breasts, cut into thin strips

200g Chinese cabbage, finely shredded

2 carrots, peeled and cut into matchsticks

4 spring onions, cut into 2.5cm pieces

300g straight-to-wok noodles

Mix the cornflour and chicken stock together in a small bowl until the cornflour dissolves. Add the garlic, soy sauce, Lea & Perrins and oyster sauce, then stir to combine. Set the sauce aside.

Heat the sesame oil in a wok or large frying pan over a high heat. Season the chicken breast strips with salt and pepper, then add to the pan. Stir-fry for 3 minutes until they have turned from pink to white, then add the cabbage, carrots and spring onions.

Continue to stir-fry for another 2–3 minutes until the vegetables have softened and the chicken is cooked through, then tip in the noodles, followed by the sauce.

Cook for a further 2 minutes, stirring, until the noodles are heated through and everything is coated in the sauce. Divide between two bowls to serve.

LEA & PERRINS ADVERTS
THROUGH THE YEARS

1989

1963

1989

THE ROYAL SEAL OF APPROVAL

In 1847, a royal chef revealed to the *Lady's Newspaper* that Lea & Perrins was a firm favourite with his employers and often served at Buckingham Palace. This was backed up a few decades later in 1904, when **King Edward VII** granted Lea & Perrins the Royal Warrant.

The sauce clearly stayed popular with the Royal Family: this photo from the 1970s shows **Prince Philip**, Duke of Edinburgh, admiring a Lea & Perrins display on a visit to Worcester.

STICKY CHICKEN WINGS

PREP 5 MINUTES
COOK 50 MINUTES

1kg free-range chicken wings, cut in half at the joint

salt and pepper

6 tbsp hot sauce (we like sriracha)

3 tbsp honey

1½ tbsp Lea & Perrins Worcestershire Sauce

Preheat the oven to 200°C/180°C fan/gas mark 6 and line a large roasting tin with baking paper.

Pat the chicken wings completely dry with the kitchen paper – this will help them crisp up. Season generously with salt and pepper.

Put the wings on to the lined tray, making sure to leave space between each one, then roast for 40–45 minutes, flipping halfway, until the wings are crisp and cooked through.

Once the wings are cooked, mix together the hot sauce, honey and Lea & Perrins in a small saucepan over a low heat. Stir until the honey has dissolved and the sauce is warm.

Put the cooked wings into a large bowl. Pour over the sauce and toss well so that each wing gets coated in the sticky glaze.

Serve with kitchen paper for sticky fingers and a bowl for the bones.

Lea & Perrins is popular with the British Army: in the First World War, troops were assured that 'Lea & Perrins makes bully beef appetising'. **Yum!**

In the Second World War, a bombing raid caused some damage to the printers who created the iconic orange Lea & Perrins labels. For a brief period, the sauce went out with a temporary black-and-white label that read: 'Messrs. Lea & Perrins are compelled to issue this label owing to the destruction of their printer's establishment by enemy action.'

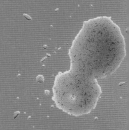

In 1964, a disastrous fire tore through the Lea & Perrins factory – but within ten days, they were back up and running, making sure the nation could still enjoy its favourite **Worcestershire sauce!**

MAKES 12

PARMESAN STRAWS

PREP 15 MINUTES, PLUS 20 MINUTES CHILLING
COOK 15 MINUTES

100 Parmesan, roughly grated
2 tbsp Lea & Perrins
   Worcestershire Sauce
320g ready-rolled puff pastry
1 medium free-range egg

Line a large baking tray with baking paper.

In a small bowl, mix together 75g of the Parmesan with the Lea & Perrins.

Unravel the sheet of puff pastry so that the shorter side is towards you. Scatter the Parmesan mixture over the top half of the pastry sheet, then fold the empty bottom half of the pastry over the top to seal the cheese inside.

Using a sharp knife, cut the pastry into 12 thin, even strips. Next, using clean hands, twizzle each pastry strip into a spirally straw shape. Place these carefully on the baking tray and transfer to the fridge for 20 minutes to chill and firm up.

Preheat the oven to 200°C/180°C fan/gas mark 6.

Crack the egg into a small bowl and whisk well with a fork. Brush the egg over the chilled pastry straws, then sprinkle over the remaining Parmesan. Bake for 12–15 minutes until crisp and deeply golden brown. Leave to cool for at least 10 minutes before eating.

The Parmesan straws will happily keep for 3–4 days in an airtight container.

SUMMERY STEAK SANDWICHES

SERVES 4

PREP 5 MINUTES
COOK 5 MINUTES

2 good-quality sirloin steaks
   (about 225g each)
3 tbsp olive oil
salt and pepper
450g jar roasted peppers,
   drained and peppers
   chopped
2 tbsp capers, drained and
   chopped
zest and juice of ½ lemon
1 tbsp Lea & Perrins
   Worcestershire Sauce
4 tbsp Heinz [Seriously] Good
   Mayonnaise
2 large ciabattas, halved and
   cut in half, or 4 ciabatta
   rolls, halved
60g rocket

Remove the steaks from the fridge 30 minutes before you begin cooking to allow them to come up to room temperature.

Rub each steak with ½ tablespoon of the oil and season generously with salt and pepper.

Heat a large non-stick frying pan over a high heat until searingly hot, then lay in the steaks. Fry to your liking (2 minutes on each side for medium-rare). Once cooked, transfer the steaks to a plate and leave to rest while you make the salsa.

In a small bowl, mix together the peppers, capers, lemon zest and juice, and Lea & Perrins with the remaining 2 tablespoons of olive oil. Season the salsa to taste.

Finely slice the steaks and sprinkle with salt, then assemble the sandwiches.

Spread the mayonnaise across the bottom halves of the ciabatta. Top with the rocket and spoon over the salsa (don't worry if there's too much to fit in the sandwiches; you can serve the rest on the side), then add the sliced steak. Sandwich together with the ciabatta tops, and serve.

GARLIC & CHILLI BUTTER PRAWNS

PREP 5 MINUTES
COOK 5 MINUTES

125g salted butter
6 fat garlic cloves, finely sliced
2 red chillies, finely sliced
1kg sustainably sourced raw
   shell-on king prawns
zest and juice of 1 lemon
1 tbsp Lea & Perrins
   Worcestershire Sauce
handful of parsley, roughly
   chopped (stalks and all)
warm crusty bread, to serve

Melt the butter in a large frying pan over a medium heat. Add the garlic and chillies and cook, stirring, for 1 minute until the garlic is lightly golden. Chuck in the prawns and cook for a further 3–4 minutes, tossing them in the garlic butter occasionally, until the shells have turned from grey to completely pink.

Take the pan off the heat and stir in the lemon zest and juice, along with the Lea & Perrins and parsley. Scrape into a serving bowl, and serve at the table with warm crusty bread for dunking and a bowl for the empty shells.

Here in the UK, Lea & Perrins comes in two bottle sizes, **150ml** and **290ml**. Some countries love it so much that they have an extra-large **568ml** bottle!

The factory has played host to many special guests over the years, including top chef **Jamie Oliver.**

Lea & Perrins is so popular that it is now exported to countries all over the world, including *Canada, Australia, the Philippines, South Africa, Kenya, Nigeria, India, Venezuela, Thailand and Japan.*

Each year, the Lea & Perrins factory produces **28 million bottles** of **Lea & Perrins** and uses **200 tonnes** of **anchovies**, **40 tonnes** of **garlic** and **125 tonnes** of **onions!**

PRAWN TACOS

PREP 5 MINUTES, PLUS
20 MINUTES MARINATING
COOK 5 MINUTES

1 fat garlic clove, crushed

1 tbsp olive oil

zest and juice of ½ orange

1 tbsp Lea & Perrins
  Worcestershire Sauce

2 tsp ground cumin

salt and pepper

360g sustainably sourced raw
  king prawns, peeled

1 red onion, very finely sliced

juice of 1½ limes, plus lime
  wedges to serve

2 avocados, peeled, stoned
  and sliced

12 small corn or flour tortillas

½ iceberg lettuce, finely sliced

150g soured cream

In a large bowl, mix together the garlic, olive oil, orange zest and juice, Lea & Perrins and ground cumin, along with plenty of salt and pepper. Stir to combine, then add the prawns to the marinade. Leave to marinate in the fridge for 20 minutes.

Meanwhile, in a small bowl, combine the red onion with the juice of 1 lime. Add a big pinch of salt then, using clean hands, scrunch the onion into the lime juice. This will help it soften and quickly pickle. Set aside.

Squeeze the remaining lime juice over the avocado slices.

When you're ready to cook, heat the tacos according to the packet instructions, and heat a large frying pan over a high heat. Add the prawns, along with their marinade. Fry for 2–3 minutes until the prawns have turned from grey to completely pink and are beginning to char in places. Tip into a bowl.

Serve the prawns alongside the quick-pickled onions, lettuce, avocado, soured cream, tacos and lime wedges, so that everyone can build their own tacos.

COURGETTE CARBONARA

PREP 10 MINUTES
COOK 20 MINUTES

salt
200g spaghetti
2 tbsp olive oil
2 courgettes, diced
2 fat garlic cloves, finely sliced
2 medium free-range egg
  yolks
50g Parmesan, finely grated,
  plus extra to serve
2 tsp Lea & Perrins
  Worcestershire Sauce
1 tsp crushed black
  peppercorns
zest of 1 lemon

Bring a large pan of salted water to the boil. Drop in the spaghetti and cook for 1 minute less than the packet instructions.

Meanwhile, heat the olive oil in a large frying pan over a medium–high heat. Add the courgettes, along with a pinch of salt. Fry, stirring regularly, for 6–8 minutes until the courgette pieces are a deep golden brown. Reduce the heat to medium and add the garlic. Cook, stirring, for 1 minute, then turn off the heat.

In a jug, mix together the egg yolks, Parmesan, Lea & Perrins, black pepper and most of the lemon zest until well combined.

Once the pasta is cooked, reserve a mugful of the pasta water, then use tongs to lift the spaghetti straight into the courgette pan. Add the egg-yolk mixture and half of the reserved pasta water, then stir vigorously until the spaghetti is coated in a luxurious creamy sauce. The residual heat will cook the egg yolks. If the sauce looks a little too thick, stir in some more pasta water.

Divide the carbonara between two bowls, and top with the remaining lemon zest and some more Parmesan to serve.

PORK LARB

PREP 5 MINUTES
COOK 15 MINUTES

1 tbsp vegetable oil
500g good-quality pork mince
2 tbsp Lea & Perrins
  Worcestershire Sauce
juice of 2 limes
1 tbsp soft light brown sugar
1 red chilli, finely chopped
4 spring onions, finely sliced
large handful of mint, leaves
  picked
large handful of coriander,
  leaves picked
2 baby gem lettuces, leaves
  separated
50g roasted salted peanuts,
  roughly chopped

Heat the vegetable oil in a wok or large frying pan over a high heat. Tip in the pork mince and fry, breaking up the mince with the back of your spoon, for 8–10 minutes until cooked through and beginning to crisp.

Add the Lea & Perrins, along with the lime juice and sugar. Give everything a good stir. Cook for a couple more minutes, then stir through the chilli, spring onions and most of the herbs. Remove the pan from the heat.

Arrange the lettuce leaves on a large platter, and fill with the pork mixture. Top with the peanuts and remaining herbs to serve.

INDEX

1 3 5 7 9 10 8 6 4 2

Published in 2022 by Ebury Press an imprint of Ebury Publishing,
20 Vauxhall Bridge Road,
London SW1V 2SA

Ebury Press is part of the Penguin Random House group of companies
whose addresses can be found at global.penguinrandomhouse.com

Penguin
Random House
UK

Publishing Director: Elizabeth Bond
Food Photography: Haarala Hamilton
Factory Photography: Andre Pattenden (17, 22, 42–3, 54, 90–1)
Design: A2 Creative
Food Styling: Sophie Godwin
Food Styling Assistants: Bella Haycraft Mee and Jodie Nixon
Props Styling: Daisy Shayler Webb
Recipe Writer: Sophie Godwin
Project Editor: Tara O'Sullivan
Development: Kraft Heinz New Ventures

www.penguin.co.uk
A CIP catalogue record for this book is available from the British Library
ISBN 9781529148855

Printed and bound in Latvia by Livonia Print SIA

The authorized representative in the EEA is Penguin Random House Ireland,
Morrison Chambers, 32 Nassau Street, Dublin D02 YH68